The Original
Summer Bridge Activities™

Third to Fourth Grade

SBA was created by
Michele D. Van Leeuwen

written by
Julia Ann Hobbs
Carla Dawn Fisher

illustrations by
Magen Mitchell
Amanda Sorensen

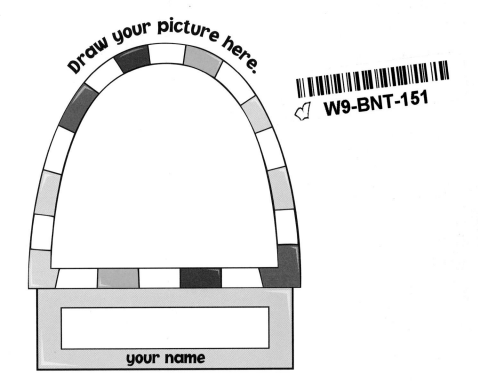

Draw your picture here.

your name

W9-BNT-151

Summer Learning Staff
Clareen Arnold, Lori Davis, Melody Feist, Aimee Hansen, Christopher Kugler,
Kristina Kugler, Molly McMahon, Paul Rawlins, Liza Richards, Linda Swain

Design
Andy Carlson, Robyn Funk

Cover Art
Karen Maizel, Amanda Sorensen

ISBN: 1-59441-729-6

Super Summer Science pages © 2002 The Wild Goose Company and Carson-Dellosa.

20 19 18 17 16 15 14 13 12 11

Dear Parents,

The summer months are a perfect time to reconnect with your child on many levels after a long school year. Your personal involvement is so important to your child's immediate and long-term academic success. No matter how wonderful your child's classroom experience is, your involvement outside the classroom will make it that much better!

Summer Bridge Activities™ is the original summer workbook developed to help parents support their children academically while away from school, and we strive to improve the content, the activities, and the resources to give you the highest quality summer learning materials available. Ten years ago, we introduced Summer Bridge Activities™ to a small group of teachers and parents after I had successfully used it to help my first grader prepare for the new school year. It was a hit then, and it continues to be a hit now! Many other summer workbooks have been introduced since, but Summer Bridge Activities™ continues to be the one that both teachers and parents ask for most. We take our responsibility as the leader in summer education seriously and are always looking for new ways to make summer learning more fun, more motivating, and more effective to help make your child's transition to the new school year enjoyable and successful!

We are now excited to offer you even more bonus summer learning materials online at www.**SummerBridgeActivities**.com! This site has great resources for both parents and kids to use on their own and together. An expanded summer reading program where kids can post their own book reviews, writing and reading contests with great prizes, assessment tests, travel packs, and even games are just a few of the additional resources that you and your child will have access to with the included Summer Bridge Activities™ Online Pass Code.

Summer Learning has come a long way over the last 10 years, and we are glad that you have chosen to use Summer Bridge Activities™ to help your children continue to discover the world around them by using the classroom skills they worked so hard to obtain!

Have a wonderful summer!

Michele Van Leeuwen and the Summer Learning Staff!

Hey Kids!

We bet you had a great school year!
Congratulations on all your hard work! We just want to say
that we're proud of the great things you did this year, and we're excited
to have you spend time with us over the summer. Have fun with your
Summer Bridge Activities™ workbook, and visit us online at
www.**SummerBridgeActivities**.com for more fun, cool, and exciting stuff!

Have a great summer!

The T. O. C. (Table of Contents)

Official Pass Code

jj0111s

Log on to www.SummerBridgeActivities.com and join!

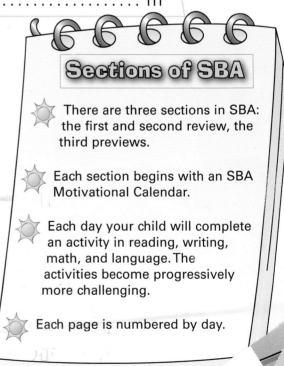

Sections of SBA

- There are three sections in SBA: the first and second review, the third previews.

- Each section begins with an SBA Motivational Calendar.

- Each day your child will complete an activity in reading, writing, math, and language. The activities become progressively more challenging.

- Each page is numbered by day.

Here's what you will find inside

Summer Bridge Activities™

Exercises in **Summer Bridge Activities**™ (SBA) are easy to understand and presented in fun and creative ways that motivate children to review familiar skills while being progressively challenged. In addition to basic skills in reading, writing, math, and language arts, SBA contains activities that challenge and reinforce skills in geography and science!

Here are some groups who say our books are great!

Daily exercises review and preview skills in reading, writing, math, and language arts, with additional activities in geography and science. Activities are presented in half-page increments so kids do not get overwhelmed and are divided into three sections to correlate with traditional summer vacation.

Bonus Super Summer Science pages provide hands-on science activities.

A Summer Reading List introduces kids to some of today's popular titles as well as the classics. Kids can rate books they read and log on to www.**SummerBridgeActivities**.com to post reviews, find more great titles, and participate in national reading and writing contests!

Motivational Calendars begin each section and help kids achieve all summer long.

Discover Something New lists offer fun and creative activities that teach kids with their hands and get them active and learning.

Grade-specific flashcards provide a great way to reinforce basic skills in addition to the written exercises.

Removable Answer Pages ensure that parents know as much as their kids!

A Certificate of Completion for parents to sign congratulates kids for their work and welcomes them to the grade ahead.

A grade-appropriate, official Summer Fun pass code gives kids and parents online access to more bonus games, contests, and resources at www.**SummerBridgeActivities**.com.

10 Ways to Maximize
The Original Summer Bridge Activities™

  First, let your child explore the book. Flip through the pages and look at the activities with your child to help him become familiar with the book.

  Help select a good time for reading or working on the activities. Suggest a time before your child has played outside and becomes too tired to do the work.

  Provide any necessary materials. A pencil, ruler, eraser, crayons, or reference works may be required.

  Offer positive guidance. Remember, the activities are not meant to be tests. You want to create a relaxed and positive attitude toward learning. Work through at least one example on each page with your child. "Think aloud" and show your child how to solve problems.

  Give your child plenty of time to think. You may be surprised by how much children can do on their own.

  Stretch your child's thinking beyond the page. If you are reading a book, you might ask, "What do you think will happen next?" or "What would you do if this happened to you?" Encourage your child to talk about her interests and observations about the world around her.

  Reread stories and occasionally flip through completed pages. Completed pages and books will be a source of pride to your child and will help show how much he accomplished over the summer.

  Read and work on activities while outside. Take the workbook out in the backyard or on a family campout. It can be fun wherever you are!

  Encourage siblings, relatives, and neighborhood friends to help with reading and activities. Other children are often perfect for providing the one-on-one attention necessary to reinforce reading skills.

Give plenty of approval! Stickers and stamps are effective for recognizing a job well done. At the end of the summer, your child can feel proud of her accomplishments and will be eager for school to start.

Skills List

Language Arts/Reading

Parent:

- ☐☐ Can write uppercase and lowercase letters in cursive
- Recognizes beginning blends:

  bl, cl, fl, gl, pl, sl, br, cr, dr, fr, gr, pr,

  tr, sk, sm, sn, sp, st, sw, tw, scr, spl, spr, str
- ☐ Recognizes r-controlled vowels: ir, ur, er, ar, or
- ☐ Recognizes diphthongs: au, aw, ew, oi, ou, ow, oy
- ☐ Recognizes compound words
- ☐ Recognizes contractions
- ☐ Recognizes silent letters in consonant combinations: kn, wr, ck, mb, tch
- ☐ Recognizes antonyms, synonyms, and homonyms
- ☐ Discriminates between nouns, verbs, adjectives, adverbs, and prepositions
- ☐ Recognizes subject and predicate
- ☐ Can divide words into syllables
- ☐ Can identify the main idea of a story
- ☐ Can identify the conclusion of a story
- ☐ Can identify cause and effect relationships in a story
- ☐ Can make predictions from context clues
- ☐ Draws illustrations to match sentences
- ☐ Uses correct punctuation
- ☐ Can use a dictionary, thesaurus, and encyclopedia
- ☐ Can identify prefixes and suffixes
- ☐ Is able to construct a short story
- ☐ Is beginning to read and write for pleasure
- ☐ Can correctly use abbreviations
- ☐ Can correctly write a friendly letter
- ☐ Can understand simple analogies

Exercises for these skills can be found inside **Summer Bridge Activities™** and can be used for extra practice. The skills lists are a great way to discover your child's strengths or what skills may need additional reinforcement.

Skills List

Math

- Recognizes odd and even numbers
- Reads and writes numbers 0 to 9,999
- Understands place value to the ten thousands place
- Knows relation and comparison symbols <, >, and =
- Can complete simple patterns
- Performs two-digit addition, with regrouping
- Performs two-digit subtraction, with regrouping
- Performs three-digit addition, with regrouping
- Performs three-digit subtraction, with regrouping
- Knows multiplication facts to 9
- Knows division facts to 9
- Can multiply one-digit numbers by two-digit numbers
- Can divide one-digit numbers into two-digit numbers without remainders
- Can divide one-digit numbers into two-digit numbers with remainders
- Can use estimation to solve problems
- Is able to solve story problems using multiplication and division
- Can sequence events
- Can write number sentences using +, −, and =
- Can read, interpret, and create a bar graph
- Can tell time in five-minute intervals
- Can estimate elapsed time to the hour
- Can measure items using standard units
- Can identify fractions to 1/10 (unit and denominator)
- Uses problem-solving strategies to complete math problems
- Can round numbers to the nearest ten
- Can count mixed amounts of money

Summertime = Reading Time!

We all know how important reading is, but this summer show kids how GREAT the adventures of reading really are! Summer learning and summer reading go hand-in-hand, so here are a few ideas to get you up and going:

Encourage your child to read out loud to you and make a theatrical performance out of even the smallest and simplest read. Have fun with reading and impress the family at the campsite next to you at the same time!

Establish a time to read together each day. Make sure and ask each other about what you are reading and try to relate it to something that may be going on within the family.

Show off! Let your child see you reading for enjoyment and talk about the great things that you are discovering from what you read. Laugh out loud, stamp your feet—it's summertime!

Sit down with your child and establish a summer reading program. Use our cool Summer Reading List and Summer Reading Program at www.**SummerBridgeActivities**.com, or visit your local bookstore and, of course, your local library. Encourage your child to select books on topics he is interested in and on his reading level. A rule of thumb for selecting books at the appropriate reading level is to choose a page and have your child read it out loud. If he doesn't know five or more of the words on the page, the book may be too difficult.

Books to Read

The Summer Reading List has a variety of titles, including some found in the Accelerated Reader Program.

We recommend parents read to pre-kindergarten through 1st grade children 5–10 minutes each day and then ask questions about the story to reinforce comprehension. For higher grade levels, we suggest the following daily reading times: grades 1–2, 10–20 min.; grades 2–3, 20–30 min.; grades 3–4, 30–45 min.; grades 4–6, 45–60 min.

It is important to decide an amount of reading time and write it on the SBA Motivational Calendar.

Use your surroundings (wherever you are) to show your child how important reading is on a daily basis. Read newspaper articles, magazines, stories, and road maps during the family vacation...just don't get lost!

Find books that tie into your child's experiences. If you are going fishing or boating, find a book on the subject to share. This will help your child learn and develop interests in new things.

Get library cards! Set a regular time to visit the library and encourage your child to have her books read and ready to return so she is ready for the next adventure! Let your child choose her own books. It will encourage her to read and pursue her own interests.

Make up your own stories! This is great fun and can be done almost anywhere—in the car, on camping trips, in a canoe, on a plane! Encourage your child to tell the story with a beginning, middle, AND end! To really challenge each other, start with the end, then middle, and then the beginning— yikes!

Summer Bridge Activities™
Summer Reading List

Fill in the stars and rate your favorite (and not so favorite) books here and online at
www.SummerBridgeActivities.com!

1 = I struggled to finish this book.
2 = I thought this book was pretty good.
3 = I thought this book rocked!
4 = I want to read this book again and again!

The Night Crossing
Ackerman, Karen

Freckle Juice
Blume, Judy

Great Kapok Tree: A Tale of the Amazon Rain Forest
Cherry, Lynne

This beautifully illustrated tale shows the creatures of the rain forest pleading with a sleeping ax-man to spare the great kapok tree.

The Courage of Sarah Noble
Dalgliesh, Alice

In Trouble with Teacher
Demuth, Patricia Brennan

Abuela
Dorros, Arthur

Nattie Parson's Good Luck Lamb
Ernst, Lisa Campbell

And Then What Happened, Paul Revere?
Fritz, Jean

Helen Keller: Toward the Light
Graff, Stewart

Queen Sophie Hartley
Greene, Stephanie

Sophie wishes she could be talented like her older siblings. Her mother reminds her that she is good at being kind. Laugh and cry along with Sophie as she struggles to develop her talent and learns to stand up for herself.

Treasure Nap

Havill, Juanita ☆☆☆☆☆

Girl from the Snow Country

Hidaka, Masako ☆☆☆☆☆

Blackberries in the Dark

Jukes, Mavis ☆☆☆☆☆

The View from Saturday

Konigsburg, E. L. ☆☆☆☆☆

No Coins, Please

Korman, Gordon ☆☆☆☆☆

Romeow and Drooliet

Laden, Nina ☆☆☆☆☆

Romeow the cat and Drooliet the dog have fallen in love with each other. Will their families (and the animal control warden) keep them apart, or will they live happily ever after?

Grasshopper on the Road

Lobel, Arnold ☆☆☆☆☆

Be a Perfect Person in Just Three Days

Manes, Stephen ☆☆☆☆☆

Can a book help you become perfect in only three days? The adventure begins when Milo Crinkly is hit in the head by a book that promises to do just that.

The Borrowers

Norton, Mary ☆☆☆☆☆

Ever wondered where those lost buttons and pins go? They are "borrowed" by creatures like Arrietty and her parents, Pod and Homily, who live under the floorboards and in the walls of houses.

Nothing Ever Happens on My Block

Raskin, Ellen ☆☆☆☆☆

Cendrillon: A Caribbean Cinderella

San Souci, Robert D. ☆☆☆☆☆

American Tall Tales

Stoutenburg, Adrien ☆☆☆☆☆

Join the SBA Kids Summer Reading Club!

Quick! Get Mom or Dad to help you log on and join the SBA Kids Summer Reading Club. You can find more great books, tell your friends about your favorite titles, and even win cool prizes! Log on to www.SummerBridgeActivities.com **and sign up today.**

Summer Bridge Activities™

Motivational Calendar

Month _____

My parents and I decided that if I complete
15 days of **Summer Bridge Activities**™ and
read _____ minutes a day, my incentive/reward will be:

_____

Child's Signature _____ Parent's Signature _____

Day 1	☆	📖	___	**Day 9**	☆	📖	___
Day 2	☆	📖	___	**Day 10**	☆	📖	___
Day 3	☆	📖	___	**Day 11**	☆	📖	___
Day 4	☆	📖	___	**Day 12**	☆	📖	___
Day 5	☆	📖	___	**Day 13**	☆	📖	___
Day 6	☆	📖	___	**Day 14**	☆	📖	___
Day 7	☆	📖	___	**Day 15**	☆	📖	___
Day 8	☆	📖	___				

Child: Color the ☆ for daily activities completed.
Color the 📖 for daily reading completed.

Parent: Initial the ___ when all activities are complete.

Discover Something New!

Fun Activity Ideas to Go Along with the First Section!

1. Set goals for your summer and post them on your refrigerator—plan fun rewards.

2. Sign up for a summer reading program at your library.

3. Look at the weather map in the newspaper and check temperatures in other cities.

4. Plan a special activity for Father's Day with your dad, a special relative, or a friend.

5. Draw a map of your neighborhood on graph paper. Chart a walk.

6. Play a game that has been put away in your closet and forgotten about.

7. Plan a reading picnic in the backyard, park, or canyon.

8. Plan a treasure hunt. Have older kids write clues for younger kids and make fun treasures.

9. Find a map of the U.S.—then map out your dream vacation.

10. Find a colony of ants. Spill some food and see what happens.

11. Make up a "Bored List" of things to do.

12. Make a graph and track the number of days the temperature rises over 90 degrees.

13. Visit a grocery store and select a "mystery" food you've never tried, like kumquats.

14. Play charades or another guessing game.

15. Take a walk around your neighborhood.

Warm-up Addition and Subtraction Problems.

Remember: The answers to addition problems are called <u>sums</u>, while the answers to subtraction problems are called <u>differences</u>.

1. 10 − 4 = 6
2. 10 − 5 = 5
3. 9 − 3 = 6
4. 7 − 5 = 2
5. 9 − 8 = 1
6. 9 − 5 = 4
7. 5 + 3 = 8
8. 10 − 8 = 2
9. 3 + 3 = 6
10. 3 + 6 = 9
11. 9 − 7 = 2
12. 6 + 4 = 10
13. 0 + 9 = 9
14. 2 + 5 = 7
15. 8 + 0 = 8
16. 7 + 3 = 10
17. 3 + 6 = 9
18. 10 − 1 = 9
19. 6 − 4 = 2
20. 6 − 2 = 4
21. 5 − 5 = 0
22. 4 + 6 = 10
23. 5 + 4 = 9
24. 2 + 7 = 9

Practice writing the letters of the alphabet in cursive.

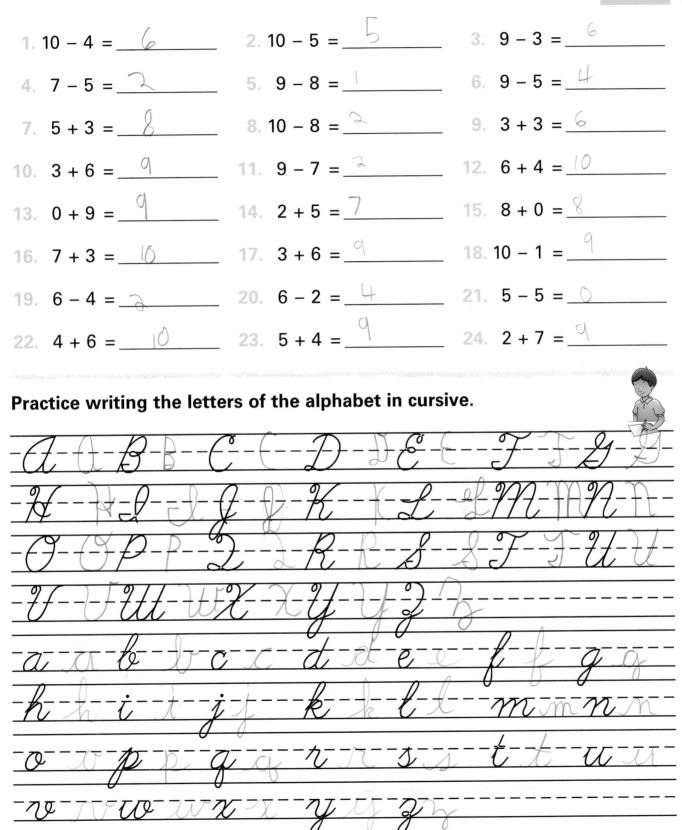

Homophones are words that sound the same but have different meanings. Write the correct word to complete the sentence.

threw
through
Their
They're
There
read
Red
two
to
too
paws
pause

1. I have __two__ more days of school.
2. Have you __read__ this book before?
3. __There__ are ninety boxes left to open.
4. That lion has large __paws__ .
5. We walked __through__ the tall grass very quickly.
6. Would you please push __pause__ on the tape player?
7. The boys had __to__ much work to do before dark.
8. __They're__ going on vacation next week.
9. Toby __threw__ the ball against the building all recess.
10. __red__ is my favorite color.
11. __their__ cousins are coming to stay for the summer.
12. We are going __too__ Lake Louise this summer.

1. Put an <u>X</u> on all the odd numbers.
2. Circle all the capital letters.
3. Put a square around the greatest number.
4. Underline in order the numbers you use to count by twos to 40.
5. Put a triangle around the number that is four less than 62.
6. Write the capital letters you circled in order, starting with the top row and moving left to right: __SUMMERFun__

b	r	q	e	o	S	c	r	y	10	6	3
U	y	10	5	2	4	M	z	1	q	a	i
6	v	0	7	8	M	p	2	10	17	12	l
r	b	14	18	b	e	16	f	h	19	E	s
18	5	14	7	2	p	m	n	z	58	20	s
94	86	22	2	R	17	l	0	24	n	x	c
26	39	3	a	d	e	28	g	h	52	19	30
7	j	F	k	32	y	34	4	31	t	10	36
0	n	e	n	38	o	80	99	U	47	x	p
w	m	m	11	N	3	14	100	c	r	e	t
q	u	v	9	7	6	w	5	40	w	13	l

Make fact families. Use the numbers in the circles.

EXAMPLE:

9 10
1

9	+	1	=	10
1	+	9	=	10
10	−	9	=	1
10	−	1	=	9

6 10
4

6	+	4	=	10
4	+	6	=	10
10	−	6	=	4
10	−	4	=	6

4 2
6

4	+	2	=	6
2	+	4	=	6
6	−	4	=	2
6	−	2	=	4

9 12
3

9	+	3	=	12
3	+	9	=	12
12	−	3	=	9
12	−	9	=	3

Practice writing these letters in cursive.

aaa aaa ccc ccc eee eee iii iii

mmm mmm nnn nnn ooo ooo

sss sss rrr rrr vvv vvv

xxx xxx wwww www uuuu uuuu

lll lll ttt ttt bbb bbb ddd ddd

kkk kkk fff fff hhh hhh

Read the story; then number the sentences in the order they happened.

FACTOID
A matchbox-sized lump of pure gold can be flattened into a thin sheet as large as a tennis court!

Every summer, my father wants to go on the same old trip that we have gone on for years. First, we pack the car full of everything we think we will need. We don't use most of it! Then we drive all night to get to Camp Busy Bee where Dad camped when he was a boy. After we get settled, everyone has to go swimming in Cool Pool. The next day we hike. On the third day, we do crafts. Last year, I made a nutcracker. It broke before I got home. On the fourth day, we go home (thank goodness).

_____4_____ On the third day, we do crafts.

_____2_____ We drive all night.

_____5_____ On the fourth day, we go home.

_____1_____ We pack the car.

_____3_____ We go swimming in Cool Pool.

Study these often misspelled words. Write them in cursive two times; then have someone read them to you while you write them.

EXAMPLE:			Now write them without looking.
1. their	*their*	*their*	1. _____
2. there	*there*	*there*	2. _____
3. until	*until*	*until*	3. _____
4. to	*to*	*to*	4. _____
5. too	*too*	*too*	5. _____
6. two	*two*	*two*	6. _____
7. unusual	*unusual*	*unusual*	7. _____
8. touch	*touch*	*touch*	8. _____
9. toe	*toe*	*toe*	9. _____
10. tear	*tear*	*tear*	10. _____

Sums and Differences through Eighteen.

14 − 9 3	13 − 5 8	9 + 8 17	9 + 9 8	15 − 8 53	11 − 7 4	16 − 8 8	12 + 3 15
7 + 5 12	8 + 8 16	12 − 6 6	15 + 3 18	18 − 9 9	5 + 6 11	12 − 7 5	11 + 6 17
18 − 9 9	4 + 8 2	11 − 4 7	15 − 9 4	13 − 8 5	14 − 6 8	7 + 9 16	17 − 8 9

Write these sentences correctly. Use capital letters and the correct punctuation. Write them in cursive.

1. our class went on a field trip to the zoo

   Our class went on a field trip to the zoo.

2. did you like the giraffe or the bear best

   Did you like the giraffe or the bear best?

3. we met a snake called sneak

   We met a snake called Sneak.

4. how long did martha stay at the zoo

   How long did Martha stay at the zoo?

Suffixes come at the end of root, or base, words. Finish these sentences by adding **-less** or **-ful** to the base word.

1. It was <u>thought**ful**</u> of Jim to bring ice cream to the picnic.

2. Mark was <u>hope **ful**</u> that he would get a part in the school play.

3. Baby puppies are <u>help **less**</u> for a few weeks.

4. Many snakes are <u>harm **less**</u> and will not hurt you.

5. We were very <u>care**ful**</u> when we crossed the river on the log.

6. I feel bad when I see <u>home **less**</u> people.

7. We had a <u>fright**ful**</u> experience on our vacation.

8. That tool has been very <u>use **ful**</u> to us.

9. The children have been <u>help**ful**</u> in our garden.

10. My grandfather seems <u>age **less**</u>.

Stories can be divided into two different types. <u>Fiction</u> is drawn from the imagination, and the events and characters are not real. <u>Nonfiction</u> has only facts about people, places, subjects, and events that are real.

Read the following paragraph and write <u>fiction</u> or <u>nonfiction</u> in the box.

> Nonfiction

Army ants are some of the most feared types of ants. These ants are very destructive and can eat all living things in their paths. Army ants travel at night in groups of hundreds of thousands through the tropical forests of Africa and South America.

Read and think. Write the problem to show how you got your answer.

EXAMPLE:

John has 18 birds. His cousin, Jim, has 9. How many more birds does John have than Jim?

__18__ ⊖ __9__ = __9__ birds

1. Carla went on a weekend trip. She took 16 pictures. Only 8 pictures turned out. How many did not turn out?

__16__ ⊖ __8__ = __8__ pictures

2. In June, I read 6 books; in July, 3; and in August, 7. How many books did I read this summer?

__6__ ⊕ __3__ ⊕ __7__ = __16__ books

3. My family and I go to the beach every year. Last year, my sister found 9 shells, my brother found 5, and I only found 4. How many shells did we find? Write the problem.

9+5+4=18

4. Dixie worked for her uncle last summer. She made $16 the first two weeks. She spent $5 to go swimming. How much did she have left? Write the problem.

16-5=11

5. In the pond, Sue counted 14 fish and 9 tadpoles. How many fewer tadpoles were there than fish? Write the problem.

14-9=5

Is it a complete sentence? Remember: A sentence is a group of words that tell a complete idea. Write yes if it is a complete sentence. Write no if it is not a complete sentence.

1. Chris slid into home plate. _yes_
2. In the top row I. _No_
3. Children watched a squirrel gather. _No_
4. The clown's funny hat fell off. _yes_
5. Pulled a wagon down. _No_
6. In the forest we saw three deer. _yes_
7. A spaceship landed by our house. _yes_
8. Our team started to. _No_
9. Mom broke a window when she was little. _yes_
10. Do you know how to do a relay? _yes_

yes

no

Read this story and fill in the blanks. Use the prefixes: <u>dis-</u>, <u>in-</u>, <u>re-</u>, and <u>un-</u>. The first one has been done for you.

dis-

in-

re-

un-

My Uncle Paul worked in a bookstore. Uncle Paul always helped me find the books I needed. He was never **dis** pleased if I asked for his help. I ____call the day I asked for a book about unsolved mysteries. Uncle Paul _____covered some on the very top of the back shelf. They were dirty and smelled dusty. They looked as if they had been ____touched for years. I started reading one about a phantom. As I looked ____side, I noticed that some pages were missing. They were the pages at the very end of the book. "Gadzooks and rats!" I said. "This story is ___complete. Now I'll never know who the phantom is." I must have looked pretty ____appointed because Uncle Paul tried to cheer me up. He said, "I don't mean to be ____kind, but think about it. You wanted to read about unsolved mysteries, and I think you ____covered a real clue about the phantom and the missing pages!"

Write five sentences about the picture. Use the boxes at the end of each line to number your sentences in story order. Write your story and give it a title. Be sure to use capital letters and periods.

1. _____ ☐

2. _____ ☐

3. _____ ☐

4. _____ ☐

5. _____ ☐

Place Value. Write the numbers.

Ex. 6 tens 8 ones **68**	1. 9 ones 4 tens *49*	2. 5 tens 0 ones *50*	3. 10 tens 0 ones *10*
4. 6 tens 3 hundreds 8 ones *368*	5. 4 hundreds 0 tens 2 ones *402*	6. 5 ones 6 hundreds 7 tens *675*	7. 9 hundreds 3 ones 5 tens *953*

Write these numbers.

8. five hundred sixty-one *561*

9. four hundred eighty-six *486*

10. two hundred ninety-nine *299*

11. eight hundred *800*

12. one hundred fifty *150*

How many gumballs in each set?

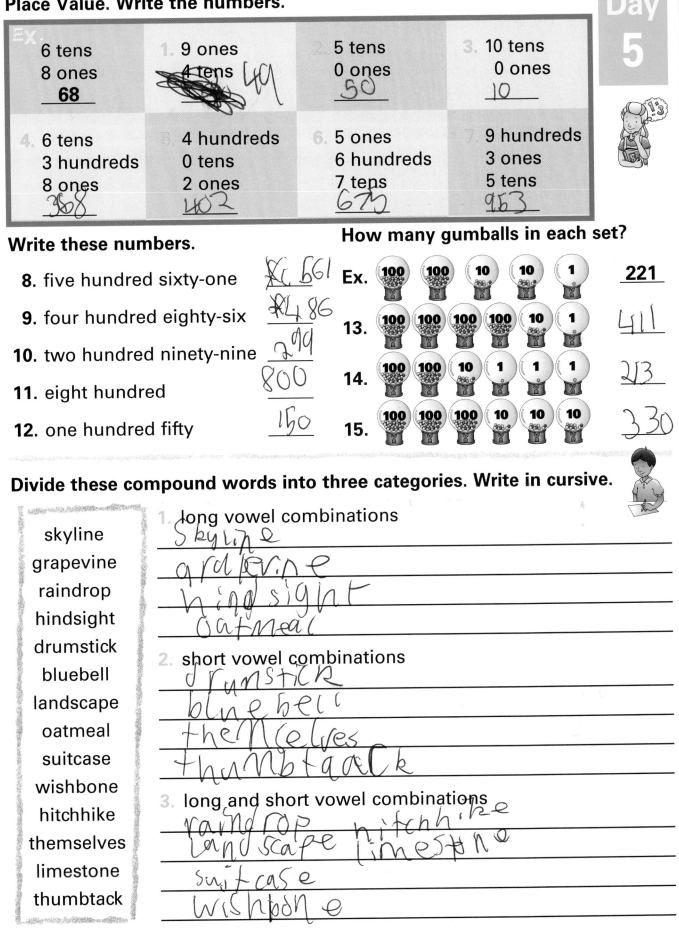

Ex. 100 100 10 10 1 **221**

13. 100 100 100 100 10 1 *411*

14. 100 100 10 1 1 1 *213*

15. 100 100 100 10 10 10 *330*

Divide these compound words into three categories. Write in cursive.

skyline
grapevine
raindrop
hindsight
drumstick
bluebell
landscape
oatmeal
suitcase
wishbone
hitchhike
themselves
limestone
thumbtack

1. long vowel combinations

Skyline
grapevine
hindsight
oatmeal

2. short vowel combinations

drumstick
bluebell
themselves
thumbtack

3. long and short vowel combinations

raindrop hitchhike
landscape limestone
suitcase
wishbone

Write a word for each clue.

knead	sense	praise	dull	guide
wheat	purchase	numb	certain	amazing

1. not able to feel _____
2. we do this to dough _____
3. to be sure _____
4. to buy something _____
5. to see, hear, feel, taste, smell _____
6. flour is made from _____
7. a leader of a group _____
8. to say something nice _____
9. something wonderful can be _____
10. a knife that is not sharp _____

Haiku is a form of Japanese poetry that follows a special pattern of 17 syllables. There are 5 syllables in the first line, 7 in the second line, and 5 in the third line. Most haiku poetry is about nature.

Read the following haiku poem.

Flakes of snow outside.
Icicles hanging from eaves.
Winter is now here.

Use the lines to write a haiku poem of your own about apples, summer, or anything you want.

_____

_____

_____

How many ways can you make the amount of money shown in these problems? Use real money to help you.

EX. **10¢**
10 pennies
2 nickels
1 nickel, 5 pennies
1 dime

2. **$1.00**
100¢
MOW the Lean
4 qharters
50 niches
w dime

3. **$1.60**
160 pennie
1 dollar
60 pennie

1. **25¢**
1 qharter
5 nickes
25 pennie

Circle the nouns Underline the verbs. Remember: Nouns name things, and verbs show action.

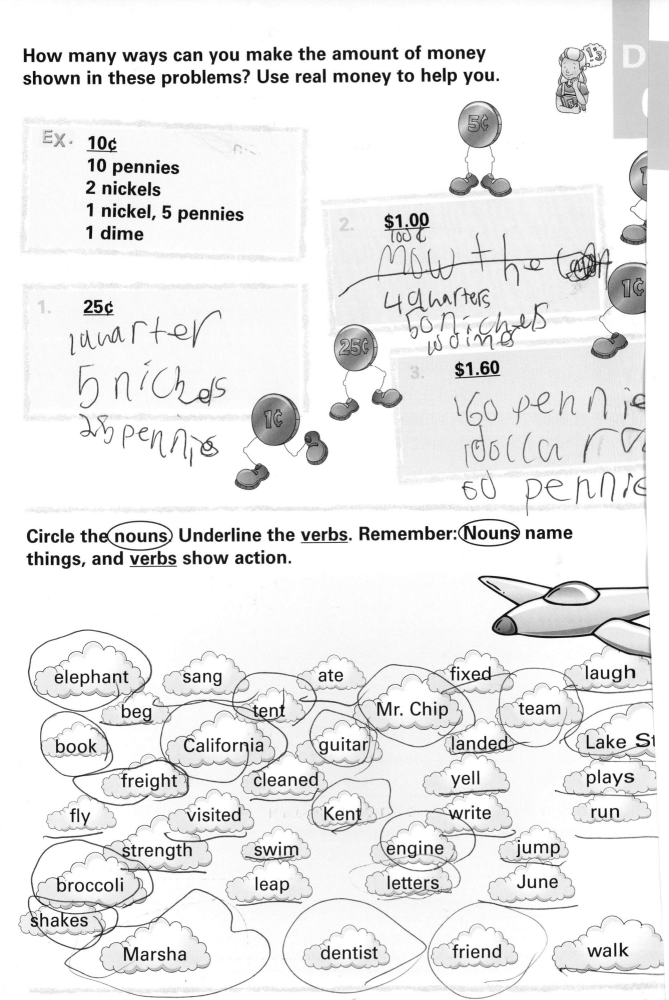

elephant   sang   ate   fixed   laugh

beg   tent   Mr. Chip   team

book   California   guitar   landed   Lake St

freight   cleaned   yell   plays

fly   visited   Kent   write   run

strength   swim   engine   jump

broccoli   leap   letters   June

shakes

Marsha   dentist   friend   walk

Use the Word Bank to make compound words matching the descriptions.

Word Bank

~~bath~~	apple
team	storm
horse	~~tub~~
snow	back
scare	side
post	card
hill	mates
pine	crow

Ex. A place your mom sends you to get clean. _bathtub_

1. A fruit that is good to eat. _apple_

2. What farmers put in cornfields to scare birds away. _scarecrow_

3. A kind of weather some people get in the wintertime. _snowstorm_

4. If you ride on a horse, you have this kind of ride. _horseback_

5. A place that might be grassy, high up, and a good place for a picnic. _hillside_

6. A type of mail you can write and send to a friend. _e-mail_

7. People who play sports with you. _teammate_

You are lost in the forest for a long time with nothing but a knife, a few matches, and one pan. How and where will you live? What will you do? What will you eat?

_____
_____
_____
_____
_____
_____
_____
_____
_____
_____
_____
_____
_____
_____

Rounding Numbers. Round to the nearest ten.

EXAMPLE:

28 = 20 or (30)
30, because 28 is nearer to 30 than to 20.

65 = 60 or (70)
70, because when a number is halfway, round it up to the larger number.

12 = (10) or 20
10, because 12 is nearer to 10 than it is to 20.

```
|----|----|----|----|----|----|----|
0   10   20   30   40   50   60   70
```

Circle the answer.

1. 63 = (60) or 70
2. 19 = 10 or (20)
3. 55 = 50 or (60)
4. 83 = (80) or 90

5. 27 = 20 or (30)
6. 99 = 90 or (100)
7. 25 = 20 or (30)
8. 12 = (10) or 20

Write the answer.

EX. 28 = **30**

9. 44 = 40
10. 13 = 10
11. 85 = 90

12. 33 = 30
13. 92 = 90
14. 78 = 80
15. 18 = 20

Round to the nearest 100.

EX. 297 = **300**

16. 211 = (200) or 300
17. 767 = 700 or (800)

18. 841 = 840
19. 587 = 600

Rewrite this paragraph. Add the correct punctuation and capitalization.

last summer we went camping in colorado we went hiking and swimming every day one time i actually saw a little deer with spots and a white tail we also collected a lot of pretty rocks flowers and leaves we had a great time i didnt want to leave

Circle the word that is divided into syllables correctly.

EXAMPLE: fi/fteen   (fif/teen)   fift/een   fifte/en

1.	cact/us	ca/ctus	cac/tus	c/actus
2.	bli/ster	blist/er	blis/ter	bl/ister
3.	al/ways	a/lways	alw/ays	alwa/ys
4.	har/bor	ha/rbor	harb/or	harbo/r
5.	fl/ower	flo/wer	flowe/r	flow/er
6.	bas/ket	bask/et	ba/sket	baske/t
7.	e/nclose	en/close	encl/ose	enclo/se
8.	obe/ys	o/beys	ob/eys	obey/s

Write the abbreviations for the following words. Be sure to put a period (.) at the end of each abbreviation. Write in cursive.

EXAMPLE:

1. January   _Jan._   2. Sunday   _____

3. February   _____ 4. Monday   _____

5. March   _____ 6. Tuesday   _____

7. April   _____ 8. Wednesday   _____

9. August   _____ 10. Thursday   _____

11. October   _____ 12. Saturday   _____

13. November   _____ 14. Doctor   _____

15. December   _____ 16. Mister   _____

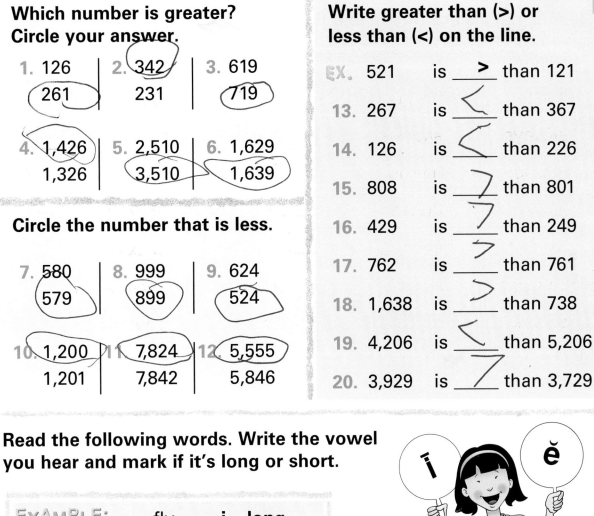

Be sure to look at the ones, tens, hundreds, and thousands as you do the following problems.

Day 8

Which number is greater? Circle your answer.

1. 126 / (261)
2. (342) / 231
3. 619 / (719)
4. (1,426) / 1,326
5. 2,510 / (3,510)
6. 1,629 / (1,639)

Circle the number that is less.

7. 580 / (579)
8. 999 / (899)
9. 624 / (524)
10. 1,200 / 1,201
11. (7,824) / 7,842
12. 5,555 / (5,846)

Write greater than (>) or less than (<) on the line.

EX. 521 is __>__ than 121

13. 267 is __<__ than 367

14. 126 is __<__ than 226

15. 808 is __>__ than 801

16. 429 is __>__ than 249

17. 762 is __>__ than 761

18. 1,638 is __>__ than 738

19. 4,206 is __<__ than 5,206

20. 3,929 is __>__ than 3,729

Read the following words. Write the vowel you hear and mark if it's long or short.

EXAMPLE:
fly — i — long
went — e — short

1. tie — i — long
2. trail — a — long
3. sweat — e — short
4. puzzle — u — short
5. chief — e — short
6. bump — u — short
7. head — e — short
8. mule — u — long
9. knot — o — short
10. niece — e — long
11. toad — o — long
12. ripped — i — short
13. bugle — u — long
14. neck — e — short
15. find — i — long
16. plan — a — short
17. high — i — long
18. chip — i — short

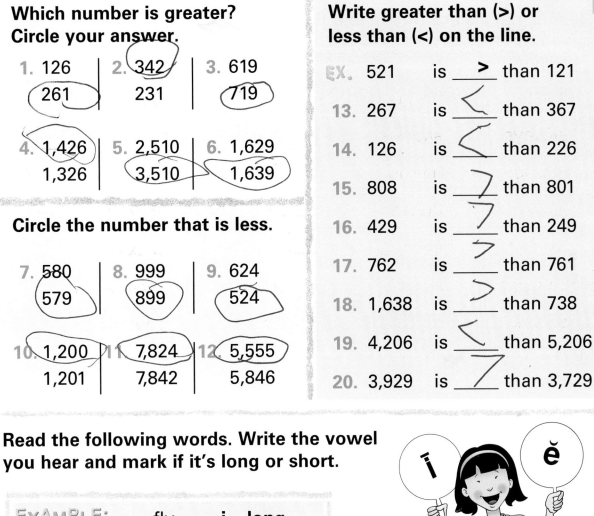

Use commas, add small words, or leave words out to combine the sentences.

EXAMPLE:

1. My friends' names are Wanda and Pete. I also like Mandy and Joe.

   I like my friends, Wanda, Pete, Mandy, and Joe.

2. Rats will chew on wood and bones. They also will chew on nuts and twigs.

   _____

3. Dogs and cats can be pets. Gerbils and hamsters can be pets, too.

   _____

4. I am wearing blue jeans and a striped shirt. My shoes are black, and my socks are green. On my head is a baseball cap.

   _____

   _____

Read the directions through completely first. If you follow the directions carefully, you will find the name of an animal.

P	L	A	E	N	H	T	E

1. Remove the letter L and the last E.
2. Put the LE at the beginning of the word.
3. Move the second E so it is at the beginning of the word.
4. Put an S at the end of the word.
5. Move the H so that it is between the P and the A.
6. Don't do step 4.
7. Write the name of the animal here.

   _____

Match the names with the shapes.

1.

2.

3.

4.

5.

6.

A. ___3___ pentagon   B. ___1___ rectangle   C. ___4___ hexagon

D. ___5___ square   E. ___6___ triangle   F. ___2___ octagon

Make real words by writing ar, ir, or, er, or ur in the blanks.

1. h_or_se   n_ur_se   th_ir_ty   p_or_ch

2. h_ar_d   ch_ir_p   s_er_ve   b_ir_ch

3. g_ir_l   th_ir_st   t_ur_key   h_er_

4. ch_ar_ge   c_ur_b   m_ar_ch   y_ar_n

5. st_or_m   b_ur_p   sp_ar_k   sk_ir_t

6. c_ir_cus   c_or_n   rep_or_t   st_ar_ch

ar

ir

or

er

ur

Build a super sandwich with the clues given and the ingredients listed.

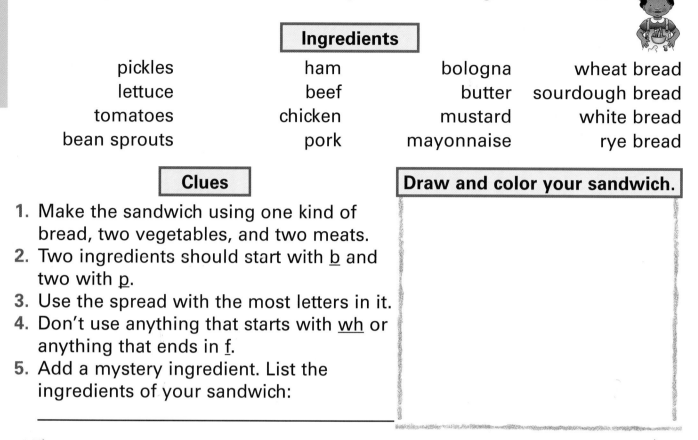

	Ingredients		
pickles	ham	bologna	wheat bread
lettuce	beef	butter	sourdough bread
tomatoes	chicken	mustard	white bread
bean sprouts	pork	mayonnaise	rye bread

Clues

1. Make the sandwich using one kind of bread, two vegetables, and two meats.
2. Two ingredients should start with <u>b</u> and two with <u>p</u>.
3. Use the spread with the most letters in it.
4. Don't use anything that starts with <u>wh</u> or anything that ends in <u>f</u>.
5. Add a mystery ingredient. List the ingredients of your sandwich:

_____

Draw and color your sandwich.

Put commas where they belong in the sentences.

EXAMPLE: August 10, 1970, and May 10, 1973, are birth dates in our family.

1. My parents were married in Portland Oregon on May 1 1959.

2. We had chicken potatoes corn gravy and ice cream for dinner.

3. George Washington became the first president on April 30 1789.

4. Sam was born June 16 1947 in Rome Italy.

5. We saw deer bear elk and goats on our trip.

6. On July 24 1962 in Boise Idaho I won the big race.

Write your own series of words in these sentences. Put in the commas.

7. My favorite desserts are _____.

8. Some of my relatives are _____.

Column Addition.

6	9	7	8	0	9	4
4	8	2	4	0	1	3
				6	9	4
+2	+3	+8	+2	+3	+2	+2
17	20	17	14	9	21	13

$6 + 1 + 2 = 9$ $2 + 6 + 1 = 9$ $1 + 0 + 8 + 0 = 9$

$7 + 3 + 5 = 15$ $8 + 9 + 8 = 25$ $7 + 2 + 5 + 3 = 17$

$3 + 4 + 8 = 15$ $3 + 1 + 4 = 8$ $6 + 3 + 2 + 1 = 12$

				32	15	73
18	41	32	25	41	30	12
20	20	11	24	12	12	62
+11	+16	+12	+20	+11	+42	+22
49	77	56	69	96	99	169

Verbs can tell what is happening now or in the past. Write a correct verb in the blank. If there is an _n_ by the blank, write a "now" verb. If there is a _p_ by the blank, write a "past" verb.

1. Two dogs (p) ___met___ each other down the road.

2. The wind (n) ___blows___ and the trees (n) ___move___ .

3. We can (n) ___win___ and (n) ___lose___ in the race.

4. Last night I (p) ___drove___ past your house.

5. The hens (p) ___ate___ at their food.

6. (n) ___grab___ the kite string, please.

7. I (p) ___laughed___ at the jokes on TV last night.

8. Yesterday, we (p) ___planted___ tulips and roses.

Fill in the blanks with words that begin with bl-, fl-, br-, cl-, sn-, gl-, st-, cr-, sk-, gr-, or sp-.

1. A big _____ _____ was in the middle of the road.
2. Sid swept the floor with a _____ after he spilled the _____ crumbs on it.
3. The _____ pole was in the middle of a _____ bed.
4. The time on the _____ gave us a _____ to the answer.
5. A _____ slithered along the cold _____.
6. Rick fixed the broken _____ with some _____.
7. The robber _____ a _____ from the_____.
8. The baby colored on her _____ with a blue _____.
9. Jane ripped her _____ as she _____ by the fence.
10. The _____ were very _____ this summer.

bl-

fl-

br-

sp- **gr-** **sk-** **cr-** **st-** **gl-** **sn-** **cl-**

Do some research on toads, frogs, and tadpoles. Use the Internet or an encyclopedia. Then, draw six pictures to show, in order, how tadpoles change into frogs or toads.

Encyclopedia

1.

2.

3.

4.

5.

6.

Write the numbers that come after, before, or between.

1. 58, _59_, 60
2. 619, _620_, _621_
3. _1,200_; 1,201
4. 80, _81_, 82
5. _887_, 888, _889_
6. 2,429; _2,430_
7. _18_, 19, 20
8. _499_, 500, _501_
9. 6,000; _6,800_
10. _16_, 17, 18
11. 209, _210_, _211_
12. _9,929_; 9,930
13. _9_, 10, _11_
14. 721, _722_, 723
15. _3,999_; 4,000
16. 151, _152_, 153
17. _305_, _306_, 307
18. 7,822; _7,823_
19. 429, _430_, _431_
20. _199_, 200, _201_
21. _7,841_, 7,842
22. 869, _870_, 871
23. 998; 999; _1,000_
24. 9,999; _10,000_

Complete each sentence using <u>more than</u>, <u>less than</u>, or <u>equal to</u>. Write your answer on the line.

Rules:

2 cups = 1 pint

2 pints = 1 quart

4 quarts = 1 gallon

EXAMPLE:

Is one cup greater than, less than, or equal to 1 pint?

If 2 cups = 1 pint,

then 1 cup is __**less than**__ 1 pint.

A. 2 pints are __=__ 1 quart.
B. 1 pint is __less__ 1 quart.

C. 3 quarts are __less__ 1 gallon.
D. 3 cups are __less__ 1 quart.

E. 1 gallon is __more__ 1 pint.
F. 6 pints are __=__ 3 quarts.

G. 2 pints are __more__ 4 cups.
H. 8 quarts are __=__ 2 gallons.

Read the paragraph and circle the answers to the questions.

Many enormous bones have been found. Scientists have put them together to make dinosaur skeletons. Fossils of other extinct animals and plants have also been found. You can see dinosaur skeletons and other fossils in many museums.

1. The main idea of the paragraph is
   a. museums.
   b. fossils.

2. The word <u>them</u> in the paragraph stands for
   a. skeletons.
   b. dinosaurs.
   c. bones.

3. The word <u>enormous</u> means
   a. huge.
   b. hungry.
   c. little.

4. In this paragraph, <u>extinct</u> means
   a. happy to be alive.
   b. not alive anymore.
   c. very big animals.

Study these words and fill in the blanks with the correct words.

night
different
dry
knock
famous
snow
hopped
walk
pear
oxygen

1. Which word begins with a silent letter?_____

2. This is a weather word._____

3. Which word has a <u>t</u> sound at the end, but it is not the letter <u>t</u> making the sound?_____

4. Which word has a silent <u>gh</u>?_____

5. Which word means "well-known"?_____

6. Which word has the short <u>o</u> sound, but the letter is not an <u>o</u>?_____

7. What do we breathe?_____

8. Which word has three syllables?_____

9. Which word sounds the same as <u>pair</u>?_____

10. A word that ends with a long <u>i</u> sound._____

See if you can figure out these story problems.

1. How many days are between the 18th and the 28th day of the month?
10 days

2. If Ted is next to last in line, and he is also tenth from the first person in line, how many children are in line?
12

3. Twenty-five children are in line. Only one is a girl. She is in the middle of the line. How many boys are in front of her, and how many are behind her?
12 in front and behind

4. There are 20 horses in a race. Prince is next to last. Name his place in the race.
14th

5. If today was the 22nd of June, what date will it be one week from today?
July June 29th

6. Jack is 16th in line. How many people are ahead of him?
15

The <u>subject</u> of a sentence tells who or what the sentence is about. The <u>predicate</u> of a sentence tells something about the subject. Both can have more than one word or just one word.

Circle the (subject) of each sentence and underline the <u>predicate</u>.

EXAMPLE:

1. (Our team) won the game.
2. (A little red fox) ran by us.
3. (Clowns) make me laugh.
4. (April) lost her house keys.
5. (We) started to swim.
6. (Lions) live in cages.
7. (Chris) worked in his garden.
8. (I) found twenty-five cents.
9. (Bees) can sting people.
10. (This ruler) is one foot long.
11. (Mom and I) rode our horses.
12. (We) went on a picnic.
13. (Chickens) lay eggs daily.
14. (Birds) make nests for their eggs.
15. (Ducks) eat lots of worms.
16. (The king) rode a bike.

Write the word that does not belong with the other words in the row. Then describe why the other words belong together.

EXAMPLE:

1. rose, daisy, lazy, tulip, lily   *lazy*   *others are flowers*

2. newspaper, book, television, magazine _____ _____

3. hand, eye, foot, hose   _____ _____

4. tuba, clarinet, jazz, flute, harp   _____ _____

5. tire, hammer, screwdriver, wrench   _____ _____

6. robin, hawk, sparrow, pig, jay   _____ _____

7. John, Tom, Robert, Jenny, Todd   _____ _____

8. Moon, Mars, Earth, Pluto, Venus   _____ _____

9. lettuce, peach, carrot, peas, beets _____ _____

10. Mary, Jane, Susan, Ann, George   _____ _____

Use the apostrophe correctly. Change each underlined word or phrase by using the apostrophe.

EXAMPLE:

1. <u>You are</u> a good piano player.   *You're*

2. This is my <u>grandmothers</u> pet dog.   _____

3. The <u>monsters</u> eyes are green.   _____

4. The boy <u>will not</u> make his bed.   _____

5. The girl <u>would not</u> help her friend. _____

6. I borrowed <u>Nancys</u> swimming suit.   _____

7. Boyd does not have a <u>catchers</u> mitt.   _____

8. <u>It is</u> so hot during the summer.   _____

Adding 2-Digit Numbers. Remember to trade or regroup.

EXAMPLE:

1 26 + 37 **63**	62 + 19 8	18 + 27 45	45 + 38 83	73 + 19 92	42 + 29 77	19 + 9 28
56 + 57 113	66 + 55 121	14 + 26 40	37 + 33 70	16 + 85 101	38 + 32 70	29 + 55 84
96¢ + 56¢ 152¢	46¢ + 64¢ 110¢	98¢ + 84¢ 182¢	95¢ + 85¢ 180¢	56¢ + 26¢ 82¢	17¢ + 17¢ 34¢	11¢ + 99¢ 110¢

Read the sentences carefully. Look at the underlined word in each sentence. Choose another word or words that mean the same as the underlined word.

EXAMPLE:

1. Will you <u>repay</u> the money I lent you? _return_
2. The oak tree is <u>afire</u>. on fire
3. Sara fell down outside, but she was <u>unhurt</u>. not hurt
4. I would like to <u>revisit</u> Disneyland sometime. come back
5. Do not <u>uncover</u> the dough, or it will dry out. take off
6. Don't use this phone; it's only for <u>incoming</u> calls. coming
7. This paper is really <u>important</u>. cracial
8. This part of the forest remains <u>untouched</u>. not touched
9. Every few years we <u>repaint</u> the school. paint again
10. I <u>dislike</u> cake and ice cream. don't like

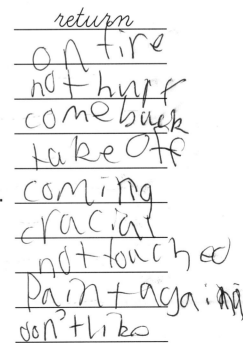

Add suffixes to the following words. Use -est, -tion, or -ty. At the end, write three sentences. Choose three different words with three different suffixes. Remember to double, drop, or change some letters.

1. taste   *tastiest*
2. act   _____
3. safe   _____
4. hungry   _____
5. prepare   _____
6. heavy   _____
7. sad   _____
8. direct   _____
9. dirt   _____
10. invent   _____

1. _____
2. _____
3. _____

Is and are tell that something is happening now. Use is with singular subjects and are with plural subjects.

1. Max and I _____ best friends.
2. Bill _____ also our friend.
3. We _____ all going camping this summer.
4. Meg _____ coming with us.
5. Her sister _____ coming, too.
6. Those bananas _____ very ripe.

is   are

Write your own sentences now. Write two using is and two using are.

1. is   _____
2. are   _____
3. is   _____
4. are   _____

Arrange the numbers from <u>greatest</u> to <u>least</u>.

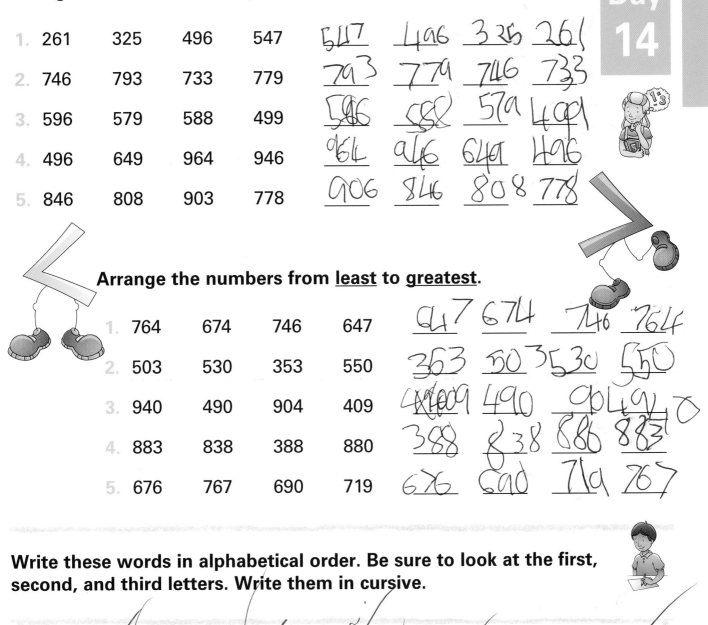

1. 261   325   496   547   _547_ _496_ _325_ _261_
2. 746   793   733   779   _793_ _779_ _746_ _733_
3. 596   579   588   499   _596_ _588_ _579_ _499_
4. 496   649   964   946   _964_ _946_ _649_ _496_
5. 846   808   903   778   _903_ _846_ _808_ _778_

Arrange the numbers from <u>least</u> to <u>greatest</u>.

1. 764   674   746   647   _647_ _674_ _746_ _764_
2. 503   530   353   550   _353_ _503_ _530_ _550_
3. 940   490   904   409   _409_ _490_ _904_ _940_
4. 883   838   388   880   _388_ _838_ _880_ _883_
5. 676   767   690   719   _676_ _690_ _719_ _767_

Write these words in alphabetical order. Be sure to look at the first, second, and third letters. Write them in cursive.

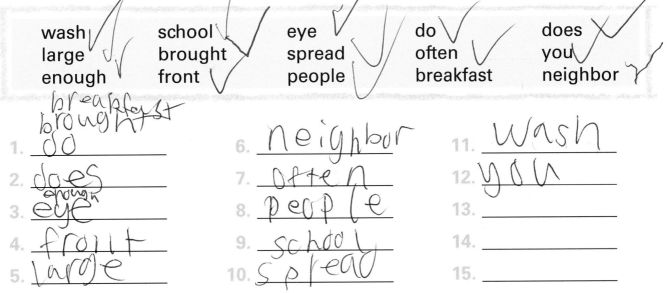

wash	school	eye	do	does
large	brought	spread	often	you
enough	front	people	breakfast	neighbor

1. _do_
2. _does_
3. _eye_
4. _front_
5. _large_

6. _neighbor_
7. _often_
8. _people_
9. _school_
10. _spread_

11. _wash_
12. _you_
13. _____
14. _____
15. _____

Day 14

Sequence.

Denise and Grayson washed their dad's car. First, they filled a bucket with soapy water. Denise got some old rags from the house while Grayson got the hose. They put soapy water all over the car and washed off the dirt. Next, they sprayed the car with water. To finish the job, Denise and Grayson wiped the car dry with some clean towels. Both of them were surprised when their dad gave them each $5.

Write four sentences about the story in the correct order.

1. _____

2. _____

3. _____

4. _____

The words below contain suffixes such as -est, -tion, and -ty. Read each one and write the base word on the line.

EXAMPLE:

1. safety _____*safe*_____

2. starvation _____

3. hungriest _____

4. action _____

5. invention _____

6. certainty _____

7. location _____

8. direction _____

9. loveliest _____

10. saddest _____

11. preparation _____

12. tasty _____

13. reality _____

14. suggestion _____

15. hottest _____

16. wettest _____

Equal Groups.

EXAMPLE:

1. Make 3 equal groups.

☆☆☆/☆☆☆☆\☆☆☆
☆☆☆/☆☆☆☆\☆☆☆

How many in each group? **7**

2. Make 5 equal groups.

How many in each group? 3

3. Make 2 equal groups.

How many in each group? 6

4. Make 4 equal groups.

How many in each group? 6

Use who's or whose in the first four blanks and you're or your in the next four.

" __Who's__ making all the racket?" shouted the king.

" __Who's__ footprints are those in the garden?"

" __Who's__ going to solve this mystery for the king?"

" __Who's__ turn is it to help the king?"

"What is __your__ favorite food?" asked the dinner guest.

"Rabbit stew!" answered the host. " __your__ going to eat it tonight for dinner."

"Great!" gulped the rabbit. " __your__ going to have to give me __you're__ recipe."

Who do you think is in the king's garden? __The rabbit__

How do you think the rabbit really felt about rabbit stew? __horrible__

Follow the directions.

1. Get a dictionary.

2. Look at any page between 40 and 55. Page_____.

3. Write down the guide words. _____, _____

4. Words in a dictionary are in _____ order.

5. Write the meaning of the guide word on the right-hand side of the page you are looking at. _____

   _____

6. How many syllables does your guide word have? _____

7. In your dictionary, what mark shows where words are divided? _____

8. Find a word on the page you are looking at that has three syllables. Write it down, and in your own words, define it. _____

   _____

9. The guide words show the _____ and the _____ entry words on the page.

Making "Clipped" Words from Longer Words. Try making these words into clipped words.

Clipped Word

EXAMPLE:

1. I can't believe that Grayson can eat four <u>hamburgers</u>!   *burgers*

2. When Andy grows up, he wants to fly <u>airplanes</u>.   _____

3. When Denise went to New York, she rode in a <u>taxicab</u>.   _____

4. A <u>hippopotamus</u> can hold its breath for a long time.   _____

5. Have you ever been inside a <u>submarine</u>?   _____

6. Spectators filled the stadium at the <u>baseball</u> game.   _____

7. Lori loves talking with her grandmother on the <u>telephone</u>. _____

8. Matt was amazed by the <u>photograph</u> in the art gallery.   _____

Card Bridge

How are your bridge construction skills? Let's see if you can build a bridge between two books with an index card. Then let's see how your bridge destruction skills are. Can you blow the bridge down?

Stuff You Need:

2 thick books
index card

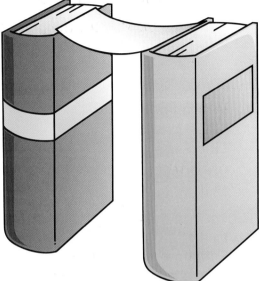

Here's What to Do:

1. Put your big books about 4 inches apart on a table. Put the index card on top of the books so that just the ends rest on the books and the rest of the card is over the open space.

2. What will happen when you blow between the two books and underneath the card? Either the card will remain unchanged, it will fly off the books, or it will bend down toward the table.

What's This All About?

Blowing below the card creates a low pressure area. The card gets pushed, not sucked, downward.

More Fun Ideas to Try:

What happens to the cloth top on a convertible car as it goes down the road is different. As the car moves down the road, the air inside the car is still, but the air outside the car is zipping across the top. The air inside is at a higher pressure than the air outside. The top is pushed upward by the air inside the convertible.

I Can't Believe My Eyes

An optical illusion is a picture that fools your eyes. Here are three different optical illusions for you to work with. Follow the model for each one, answer the questions, and create new models.

Stuff You Need: pencil, ruler

Here's What to Do:

1. Which line is shorter? _____
   Line 1 is exactly _____ millimeters long.
   Line 2 is exactly _____ millimeters long.

   What do you think makes this optical illusion work? _____
   Make an illustration similar to this illusion on a sheet of paper.

2. Look at the illustration. Is the box "coming out of the page" upward and to the left, or down and to the right? _____
   Explain how you could tell. _____
   Take a survey of your family members to see which side of the box they think is coming out of the page.

3. Look at the picture on the right. Do you see a young lady or an older woman? Tell where the young lady is looking and where the old lady is looking.

What's This All About?

An optical illusion is a drawing or image that makes your brain interpret data in a certain way. Your brain takes the image seen by each eye and makes them one image. Your brain also likes patterns—definite identification of images—which is why it is hard to see the old and young lady at the same time.

More Fun Ideas to Try:

1. If you have access to the Internet, get an adult's help to search for other optical illusions.

2. Perhaps you can take a field trip to a local art store and look for the colorful images that have hidden pictures in them (sometimes referred to as "magic eye"). Can you see the hidden images? When you are looking, be patient, stand still, and let your vision blur slightly, as if you are looking through the picture at something else far away. If you still can't see the hidden images, do some research about why some people cannot see them (again, the Internet is a good place to start).

Motivational Calendar

Month

My parents and I decided that if I complete
20 days of **Summer Bridge Activities**™ and
read _____ minutes a day, my incentive/reward will be:

Child's Signature _____ Parent's Signature_____

Day 1	☆	📖	____	Day 11	☆	📖	____
Day 2	☆	📖	____	Day 12	☆	📖	____
Day 3	☆	📖	____	Day 13	☆	📖	____
Day 4	☆	📖	____	Day 14	☆	📖	____
Day 5	☆	📖	____	Day 15	☆	📖	____
Day 6	☆	📖	____	Day 16	☆	📖	____
Day 7	☆	📖	____	Day 17	☆	📖	____
Day 8	☆	📖	____	Day 18	☆	📖	____
Day 9	☆	📖	____	Day 19	☆	📖	____
Day 10	☆	📖	____	Day 20	☆	📖	____

Child: Color the ☆ for daily activities completed.
Color the 📖 for daily reading completed.

Parent: Initial the ____ when all activities are complete.

Discover Something New!

Fun Activity Ideas to Go Along with the Second Section!

1. Find a pen pal; send him/her a letter.

2. Check if garden peas are ripe.

3. Arrange photo albums.

4. Make fruit juice bars and freeze them.

5. Learn sign language or Morse code.

6. Play capture the flag under a full moon.

7. Visit a ghost town.

8. Plan a bike hike with your family.

9. It's a great day for a family or neighborhood water fight!

10. Select a topic of interest—go to the library and check out three books on the topic.

11. Build a small wooden boat and use it during a gutter-gushing thunderstorm.

12. Get a discount pass to a local baseball or softball game.

13. Weed a row in the garden. (Mom and Dad will love you for it!)

14. Eat some French fries—learn a French phrase: s'il vous plaît.

15. Research some trivia—collect some information at the library and surprise your family.

16. Visit a local children's museum.

17. Do something ecological—clean up an area near your house. Make your planet better.

18. Collect twenty assorted bugs and identify them.

19. Go to a planetarium and see a star show.

20. Take time to paint the fence. (Ever heard of Tom Sawyer?)

Find the differences. Be sure to trade or regroup.

EXAMPLE:

7 10	6 12					
8̸0̸	7̸2̸	64	23	70	43	77
− 29	− 7	− 57	− 9	− 23	− 14	− 28
51	**65**					

63	91	38	81	55	82	25
− 45	− 42	− 19	− 15	− 9	− 16	− 16

68	76	75	85	50	31	44
− 39	− 37	− 7	− 17	− 24	− 15	− 36

Go to the library and get a book you have not read. After you finish reading it, write a book report. Use the outline below to help you.

1. Title _____

2. Author _____

3. Main characters_____

   _____

4. Setting: Where does the story take place? _____

5. Main idea: What is the book about? _____

   _____

   _____

   _____

6. Did you like the book? _____ Why or why not? _____

   _____

   _____

Complete the story web. Use the words in the web to write a story on a separate piece of paper. Be sure to use capital letters and periods. Think of a cool title for your story.

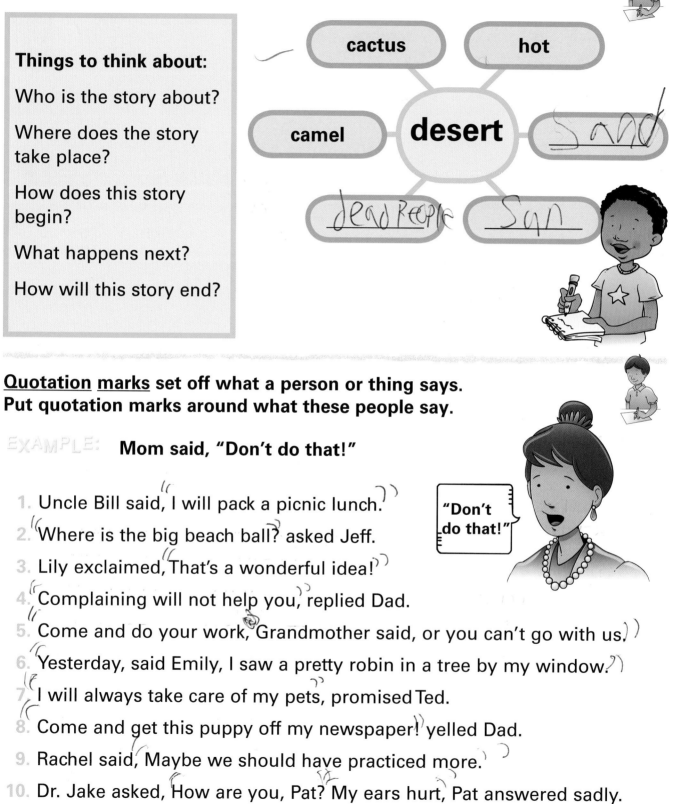

Things to think about:

Who is the story about?

Where does the story take place?

How does this story begin?

What happens next?

How will this story end?

cactus   hot

camel   **desert**   sand

dead people   sun

Quotation <u>marks</u> set off what a person or thing says.
Put quotation marks around what these people say.

EXAMPLE: **Mom said, "Don't do that!"**

"Don't do that!"

1. Uncle Bill said, "I will pack a picnic lunch."

2. "Where is the big beach ball?" asked Jeff.

3. Lily exclaimed, "That's a wonderful idea!"

4. "Complaining will not help you," replied Dad.

5. "Come and do your work," Grandmother said, "or you can't go with us."

6. "Yesterday," said Emily, "I saw a pretty robin in a tree by my window."

7. "I will always take care of my pets," promised Ted.

8. "Come and get this puppy off my newspaper!" yelled Dad.

9. Rachel said, "Maybe we should have practiced more."

10. Dr. Jake asked, "How are you, Pat?" "My ears hurt," Pat answered sadly.

Using Grids.

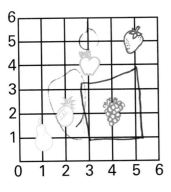

Which fruit is located at 3, 4? ___apple___

Put a circle around the fruit located at 2, 2.

Draw a peach on 5, 3.

Which fruit is located at 5, 5? ___strawberry___

Where is the pear located? ___1, 1___

Put a box around the fruit located at 4, 2.

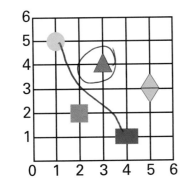

Which shape is located at 5, 3? ___diamond___

Where is the square located? ___2, 2___

Draw a circle around the shape located at 3, 4.

Draw a line to connect the shapes located at 4, 1 and 1, 5.

<u>Common nouns</u> are general names for places, things, and people. <u>Proper nouns</u> name a specific person, place, or thing and begin with a capital letter.

EXAMPLE:

Put these nouns under the right heading and then write two of your own. Be sure to use capital letters on the proper nouns.

salt lake	dog	
monday	ocean	
pet	oak street	
day	class	
november	holiday	
mr. brown	christmas	
boston	boat	
beans	rex	
apple	florida	
school	dr. phil	

Proper Nouns	**Common Nouns**
1. Mrs. Jones	1. teacher
2. Salt lake	2. zoo
3. Monday	3. ocean
4. Oak street	4. pet
5. November	5. day
6. Mr. Brown	6. class
7. Christmas	7. hol day
8. Boston	8. boat
9. Rex	9. beans
10. Florida	10. apple
11. Dr. Phil	11. school
12.	12.

Read this paragraph and then answer the questions.

Before you decide what kind of pet you would like to own, there are some things you need to think about. First, you need to find out how much care the pet would need. Dogs need to be walked; horses need to be exercised; cats need a place to scratch. All pets need to be kept clean and well fed. You need to think about where your pet would live. Big pets need a lot of room, while little pets don't need as much room.

1. What is the topic?
   a. caring for a dog
   b. choosing a pet
   c. feeding big pets

2. What is the main idea?
   a. finding a good home for pets
   b. things to do when choosing a pet
   c. things to think about before choosing a pet

3. What pet do you own or would you like to own? _dog_____

Read these silly sentences and then make your own silly sentences. Try to use the same starting letter for most of the words.

1. Silly Sandra sells sweet sandwiches sprinkled with sugar.
2. Bill Benson built a boat with beetle–bitten birch bark.

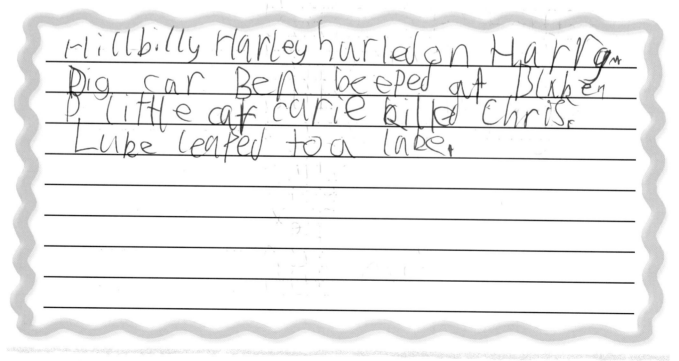

Hillbilly Harley hurled on Harry.
Big car Ben beeped at Blaken
little cat carie bit Chris.
Luke leafed to a lake.

Add or subtract. Check the signs. Trade or regroup if you need to.

EXAMPLE:

1	5 12				
$8.54	$6.25	$7.42	$8.70	$3.69	$9.60
+ 1.60	− 1.84	− 1.16	− 6.30	− 1.25	+ 1.92
$10.14	$4.41				

575	600	804	133	202	623
− 162	+ 197	+ 129	− 124	− 102	+ 527

289	211	555	475	758	908
+ 428	+ 429	− 326	+ 482	− 523	+ 129

Discover the secret message by starting with the letters in the first vertical row. Record each letter in that row in order from top to bottom; then do the same thing with the remaining rows.

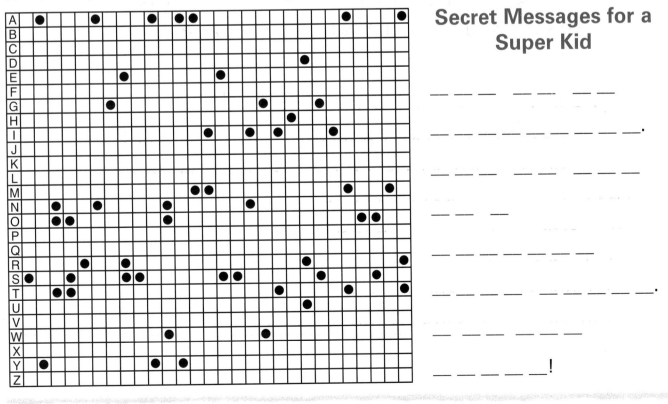

Secret Messages for a Super Kid

___ ___ ___ ___ ___ ___ ___

___ ___ ___ ___ ___ ___ ___ ___ ___.

___ ___ ___ ___ ___ ___ ___ ___

___ ___ ___

___ ___ ___ ___ ___ ___ ___

___ ___ ___ ___ ___ ___ ___ ___.

___ ___ ___ ___ ___ ___ ___

___ ___ ___ ___ ___!

Sequencing. Read this story; then number the sentences in the order they happened.

Pow

Last summer on our way to camp, the bus broke down. Our driver was able to get the bus off the road before it stopped. We were asked to stay on the bus and sit quietly in our seats. We stayed in our seats, but we were not quiet. We sang camp songs and camp chants that we learned at camp the year before.

A policeman came by and called for help on his radio. It took about an hour before another bus came to take us the rest of the way. It was a newer bus, and it wasn't long before we were choosing what bed we were going to sleep in instead of what seat we were going to sit in on the bus.

☐ We sang songs and chants while waiting for another bus.
☐ Our bus broke down on our way to camp.
☐ Another bus came by to take us to camp.
☐ We chose what bed to sleep in.
☐ A policeman came by and radioed for help.

Here are some often misspelled words. Practice them; then spell them to a friend. Be sure to write in cursive. Write each word at least four times.

wonderful _____

warm _____

worried _____

who _____

where _____

weigh _____

want _____

won't _____

was _____

word _____

Day 4

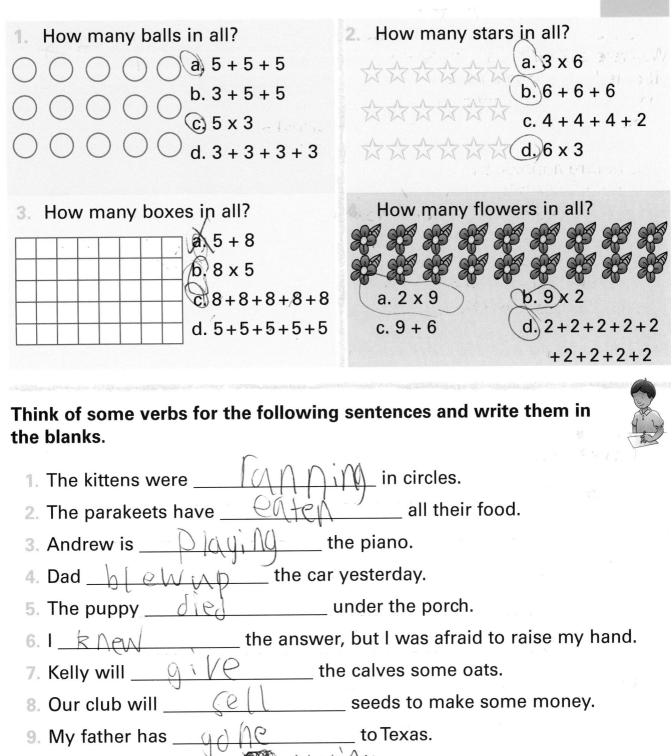

1. How many balls in all?
   - a. 5 + 5 + 5
   - b. 3 + 5 + 5
   - c. 5 x 3
   - d. 3 + 3 + 3 + 3

2. How many stars in all?
   - a. 3 x 6
   - b. 6 + 6 + 6
   - c. 4 + 4 + 4 + 2
   - d. 6 x 3

3. How many boxes in all?
   - a. 5 + 8
   - b. 8 x 5
   - c. 8 + 8 + 8 + 8 + 8
   - d. 5 + 5 + 5 + 5 + 5

4. How many flowers in all?
   - a. 2 x 9
   - b. 9 x 2
   - c. 9 + 6
   - d. 2 + 2 + 2 + 2 + 2 + 2 + 2 + 2 + 2

Think of some verbs for the following sentences and write them in the blanks.

1. The kittens were ___running___ in circles.
2. The parakeets have ___eaten___ all their food.
3. Andrew is ___playing___ the piano.
4. Dad ___blew up___ the car yesterday.
5. The puppy ___died___ under the porch.
6. I ___knew___ the answer, but I was afraid to raise my hand.
7. Kelly will ___give___ the calves some oats.
8. Our club will ___sell___ seeds to make some money.
9. My father has ___gone___ to Texas.
10. The airplane was ___landing___ at the airport.
11. Mother ___cut___ the cake into ten pieces.
12. Travis ___rides___ his bike twenty miles a week.

Choose the correct homophone to complete the sentence.

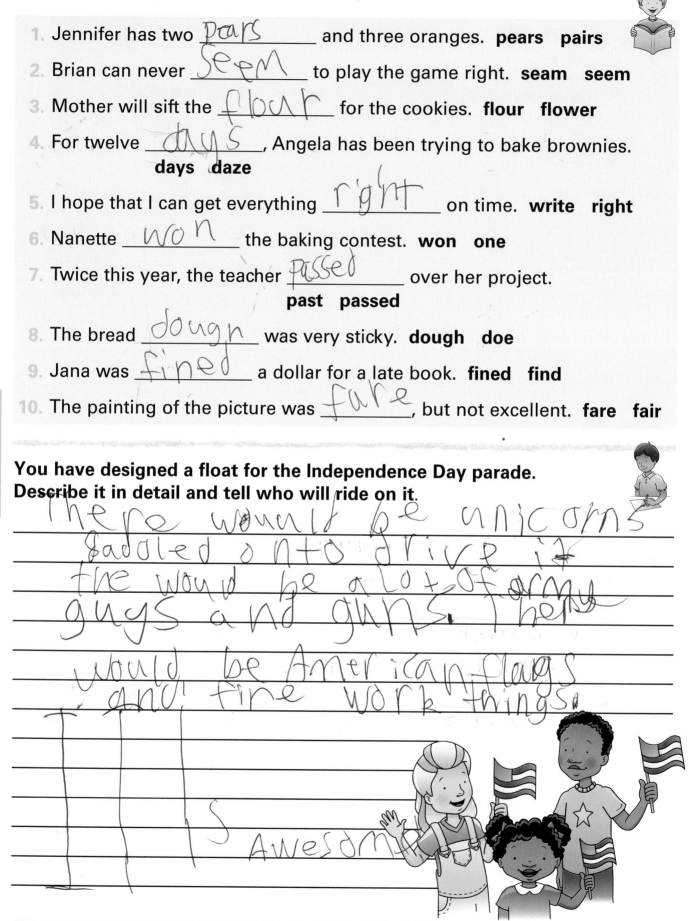

1. Jennifer has two __pears__ and three oranges. **pears   pairs**
2. Brian can never __seem__ to play the game right. **seam   seem**
3. Mother will sift the __flour__ for the cookies. **flour   flower**
4. For twelve __days__, Angela has been trying to bake brownies.
   days   daze
5. I hope that I can get everything __right__ on time. **write   right**
6. Nanette __won__ the baking contest. **won   one**
7. Twice this year, the teacher __passed__ over her project.
   past   passed
8. The bread __dough__ was very sticky. **dough   doe**
9. Jana was __fined__ a dollar for a late book. **fined   find**
10. The painting of the picture was __fare__, but not excellent. **fare   fair**

You have designed a float for the Independence Day parade.
Describe it in detail and tell who will ride on it.

There would be unicorns
saddled onto drive it
the would be a lot of army
guys and guns. They
would be American flags
and fine work things.

Is
Awesome

Thinking about Time.

1. What time does the clock show? _8:30_

2. How long does it take for the minute hand to move from 6 to 5? _5 minutes_

3. What time will it be when the minute hand reaches the 12? _9:00_

4. What time will it be when the minute hand moves 15 minutes? _8:45_

Read the sentences and fill in the blanks with words that use two different sounds of ow. Then read the finished sentences aloud.

OW

ow

1. A scarecr_ow_ really works to keep birds away from the corn. A bird was here a while ago, but it has fl_ow_n away.

2. You have been playing outside and are so dirty that you need a sh_ow_er. Here is a clean washcloth and t_ow_el to use.

3. I need to use a lawn m_ow_er to cut our grass. It has gr_ow_n so tall.

4. The king wears a gold cr_ow_n on his head, and his wife, the queen, wears a beautiful g_ow_n.

5. You have food on your face just above your eyebr_ow_. Don't fr_ow_n, just wash it off!

Read this story. Then answer the questions.

One day, a lad was chopping wood in a forest. All at once, he heard a muffled sound coming from behind a tree. He stopped chopping, walked over to the tree, and peeked behind it. He could not believe his eyes. Right there, at the foot of the tree, a leprechaun was hiding a pot of gold.

1. In this story, <u>muffled</u> means
   a. quiet.
   b. to keep warm.
   c. to gag someone.

2. Another word for <u>forest</u> is
   a. big logs.
   b. a few trees.
   c. woods.

3. <u>Lad</u> is another name for
   a. girl.
   b. boy.
   c. man.

4. A word in the story that sounds like <u>herd</u> is _____.

5. The word <u>he</u> stands for
   a. the leprechaun.
   b. the tree.
   c. the lad.

Do you remember the difference between fiction and nonfiction? <u>Fiction</u> is drawn from the imagination, and the events and characters aren't real. <u>Nonfiction</u> has only facts about real people, places, subjects, and events.

Write your own story. Is it fiction or nonfiction? Why?

_____

_____

_____

_____

_____

_____

_____

Multiplication. Finish the charts.

X2	
4	
8	
3	6
6	
9	
5	10
7	

X3	
3	9
7	
5	
2	
6	18
4	
8	

X4	
10	
5	20
8	
4	
7	
6	
9	

X5	
9	
2	
6	
3	15
5	
7	
4	

**Use a word from the box to complete each sentence.
Divide the word by what you know about syllables.**

trumpet
cottage
circus
pictures
market
quarter
signal
pennies
chatter
curtains

EXAMPLE:

1. I am learning to play the __trum•pet__ .
2. Look at all the funny _____ in this book.
3. You can buy bread and milk at the _____.
4. We live in a small _____.
5. This pencil costs a _____.
6. I am saving lots of _____ in a jar.
7. The clowns at the _____ were great.
8. When you hear the _____, run fast.
9. We have white _____ on our window.
10. Chipmunks _____.

Read the paragraph and answer the questions at the end.

evil
guy→

Reading a newspaper is a fun activity. It is also an important way to learn about what's going on in the world around you. Newspapers tell you who is doing what—and often, why they are doing it. There is a weather page to tell you what the weather is going to be like the next day and probably all week. The sports section usually tells you what games are coming up and what teams won yesterday. Newspapers tell us about our world leaders and what happens in their countries. Newspapers also tell us about accidents and serious events.

Why did the author write this?

a. to give us important facts about newspapers

b. to tell us that newspapers are make-believe

c. to tell us about the weather and sports

Practice writing and spelling -ing words. Write in cursive.

starting

hiking

stopping

breathing

sneezing

blooming

breaking

speaking

hearing

listening

spelling

working

running

walking

Make up and write some of your own -ing words.

EXAMPLE:

hitting

napping

Draw a straight line through three numbers that add up to the sum given in each diagram below.

1. Sum: 78

20	28	14
16	32	42
19	18	13

2. Sum: 110

16	33	64
39	22	44
51	10	72

3. Sum: 251

71	47	18
82	20	46
98	43	33

4. Sum: 149

15	93	24
63	25	33
63	25	61

5. Sum: 506

94	100	90
88	206	58
79	200	96

6. Sum: 189

94	100	90
88	20	58
79	10	96

Use the correct form of the verb—past or present.

1. My friends and I like to _____ clay animals. **(make)**

2. We _____ the clay into different shapes. **(roll)**

3. Jeremy _____ making a clay hippo. **(enjoy)**

4. Our teacher _____ us fire the clay animals. **(help)**

5. He _____ them all in the kiln. **(place)**

6. After they were fired, we _____ them. **(paint)**

7. Often, we _____ them as gifts. **(give)**

8. We all said we would _____ them again sometime. **(make)**

These sentences are mixed up. Write them in cursive the correct way. Don't forget capitals and punctuation marks.

1. rolled hill the we down in a car _____

_____

2. was car no but hurt wreck luckily one was a the total _____

_____

_____

3. themselves elephant animals when braced all the sneezed the _____

_____

_____

4. bottles of full wagon a pulled cory _____

_____

5. book went I bed closed and my to _____

_____

Continue the counting pattern.

1.	0	3	6	9	12	___	___	___	24	___
2.	6	12	18	24	___	___	___	48	___	___
3.	12	16	20	24	___	___	___	___	44	___
4.	33	30	27	24	___	___	___	___	9	___
5.	100	98	96	94	___	___	___	86	___	___
6.	___	___	___	25	30	35	___	___	___	___
7.	7	14	21	___	___	___	49	___	___	___
8.	25	50	___	100	___	___	175	___	___	___

Temperatures are measured in Fahrenheit (F) and Celsius (C). 32 degrees Fahrenheit is equal to 0 degrees Celsius.

Write the temperature showing on the thermometer in the space below.

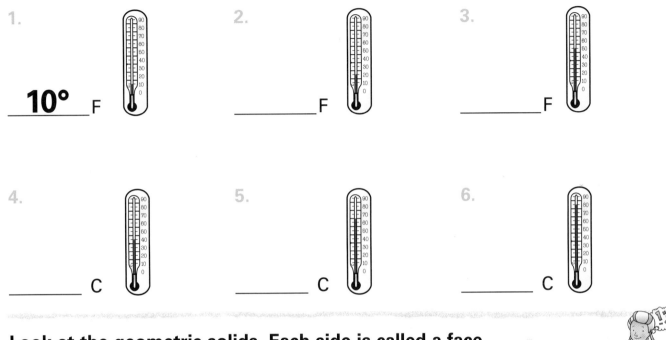

1. __**10°**__ F

2. _____ F

3. _____ F

4. _____ C

5. _____ C

6. _____ C

Look at the geometric solids. Each side is called a face. Write the number of faces each solid has.

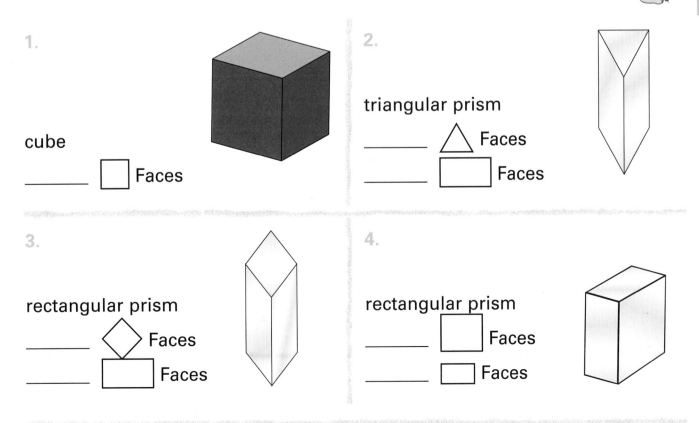

1. cube

_____ ☐ Faces

2. triangular prism

_____ △ Faces

_____ ▭ Faces

3. rectangular prism

_____ ◇ Faces

_____ ▭ Faces

4. rectangular prism

_____ ☐ Faces

_____ ▭ Faces

Draw a line to the correct ending for each sentence.

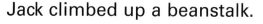

1. The teacher wrote names   was very generous to her people.
2. The girl did not want to   Jack climbed up a beanstalk.
3. In the story "The Magic Beans,"   we see many travelers.
4. The queen of Tooly Town   leave her old school.
5. North America is a   is going to hit your head.
6. What did you do with   learn responsibility for what you do.
7. In the summertime,   red handkerchief in his pocket.
8. Is a greenhouse a   on the board with chalk.
9. Sometimes you have to   very big continent.
10. The tall boy had a large,   out the secret.
11. My little sister blurted   place where you can grow plants?
12. Look out! That ball   my new rollerblades?

True or False. Read the paragraph; then fill in the blanks below. Put a <u>T</u> for true and an <u>F</u> for false.

Rain and snow provide water for our earth. When it rains or snows, water goes into the ground, streams, rivers, and other bodies of water. Little rivers run into big rivers, and big rivers run into the oceans. The sun pulls up some of the water and forms clouds. This is called evaporation. The clouds get heavy and form rain or snow that falls back to earth. This process is called the water cycle.

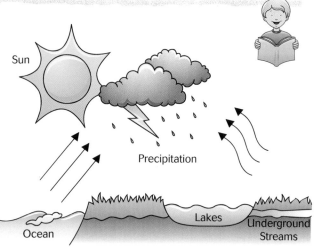

Sun
Precipitation
Ocean
Lakes
Underground Streams

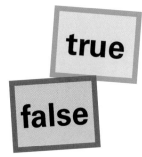

true
false

_____ 1. All living things need water.
_____ 2. Rain and snow are part of the water cycle.
_____ 3. Water is evaporated by the sun.
_____ 4. No rivers run into the ocean.
_____ 5. Clouds make the water evaporate.
_____ 6. Another name for <u>ocean</u> is <u>sea</u>.
_____ 7. All water is good to drink.
_____ 8. People pollute the water.

How Many?

1. How many 6s are there in 18? _____
2. How many 5s are there in 25? _____
3. How many 2s are there in 8? _____
4. How many 4s are there in 20? _____
5. How many 9s are there in 18? _____
6. How many 7s are there in 21? _____
7. How many 3s are there in 12? _____
8. How many 8s are there in 32? _____
9. How many 6s are there in 24? _____
10. How many 1s are there in 70? _____

Whoa! I'm multiplying!

Read the sentences and mark whether the underlined word is spelled right or wrong.

	Right	Wrong
EXAMPLE:		
That was an <u>unnkind</u> thing to say.	_____	X
1. <u>I'd</u> like a glass of water.	_____	_____
2. Do you know where <u>theyv'e</u> been today?	_____	_____
3. Be <u>carefull</u> with that knife.	_____	_____
4. My mom was very <u>unhappy</u> today.	_____	_____
5. What did Joan plant in her <u>gardin</u>?	_____	_____
6. We looked at all the <u>babyies</u> in the hospital.	_____	_____
7. Aunt Mary bottled ten pounds of <u>cherries</u>.	_____	_____
8. He waved at us from the <u>window</u>.	_____	_____
9. Dad bought a big <u>balluen</u> for my little sister.	_____	_____
10. The deer ate <u>allmost</u> all of our bushes last winter.	_____	_____

Read the story. Write complete sentences for your answers.

Robert and Sydni are two of my very best friends. We have gone to school together since we were in kindergarten. We even go to summer camp and the recreation center together. There are many reasons why I like to be with them. Robert always lets me borrow his skateboard. He knows that if I had a skateboard, I would let him borrow it. Robert is a person you can count on, too. When we are out riding our bikes together, Sydni sometimes has me ride in front while she rides behind me. She understands that the way to be a good friend is by taking turns and being fair.

1. What is it that Robert does to be a good friend?

_____

_____

2. Is Sydni a fair person? Why?

_____

_____

3. List three things that the friends do together.

_____

_____

_____

_____

4. Write a few sentences of your own about what you think makes a good friend.

_____

_____

_____

_____

_____

_____

Story Problems.

1. Nancy weighs 43 pounds. Janet weighs 34 pounds. How many pounds do they weigh together? _____

2. Bill threw 259 balls, and Kirk only threw 137. How many more balls did Bill throw than Kirk? _____

3. Jake collected 694 marbles. Joyce collected 966. How many fewer marbles did Jake collect than Joyce? _____

4. Mary Ann has a stack of 42 cards. She wants to divide them into 6 equal stacks. How many will she have in each stack? _____

Match the geometry terms with their definitions.

1. parallel lines

      lines that never intersect

      lines that intersect to form four right angles

2. perpendicular lines

      a flat surface of a solid figure

3. vertex

      a line segment where two or more faces of a solid figure meet

4. face

      the endpoint of three line segments on a solid figure

5. edge

      the space between two nonparallel rays that share an endpoint

6. ray

      lines that cross each other at only one point

7. line segment

      a line with two endpoints

8. angle

      a line that has one endpoint and continues on in one direction

9. intersecting lines

Circle the letter to answer the question and then divide the underlined word into syllables.

1. A <u>chipmunk</u> is about the size of a gerbil.
   <u>Chipmunk</u> means   a. plant   b. bug   c. animal

2. Richard <u>collects</u> stamps.
   <u>Collect</u> means   a. save   b. give away   c. licks

3. The cows will <u>produce</u> lots of milk this summer.
   <u>Produce</u> means   a. drink   b. eat   c. give

4. Anna had lots of <u>spangles</u> on her party dress.
   <u>Spangles</u> means   a. bright objects   b. dull objects   c. paper

5. The tires on the car left an <u>imprint</u> on the grass.
   <u>Imprint</u> means   a. mark   b. oil   c. water

6. Some baby <u>goslings</u> were in our pond.
   <u>Goslings</u> are   a. young geese   b. old geese   c. young chickens

How Do Seeds Grow? Write down the conditions that are necessary for seeds to germinate and grow.

Multiply.

6	5	9	9	3	8	9	6
x 4	x 2	x 7	x 0	x 5	x 4	x 6	x 5

1 x 7 = _____	6 x 8 = _____	3 x 8 = _____
3 x 2 = _____	2 x 7 = _____	7 x 7 = _____
4 x 4 = _____	8 x 8 = _____	1 x 9 = _____
5 x 9 = _____	3 x 3 = _____	5 x 5 = _____

1	9	6	0	9	2	5	0
x 8	x 2	x 6	x 7	x 9	x 2	x 5	x 0

Make each underlined word mean more than one (plural) and write it in the blank.

EXAMPLE:

1. One baby <u>calf</u> plus one more makes two baby ___*calves*___.

2. The <u>wolf</u> howled until two _____ howled with him.

3. She put a book on a <u>shelf</u> and put all the other books on the rest of the _____.

4. The blacksmith put a horseshoe on the horse's <u>hoof</u>, and then he put the others on the rest of the _____.

5. The <u>child</u> played alone until the other _____ came.

6. He left his <u>wife</u> with all the other _____ at the meeting.

**Choose a word from the Word Bank that fits each meaning.
Then write it in the puzzle.**

Down

2. very, very sad
4. spin around and around
6. making something look larger
8. very sure of something
10. not better

Across

1. need to do it right now
3. send back to the store
5. take care of the sick
7. to go after
9. the earth

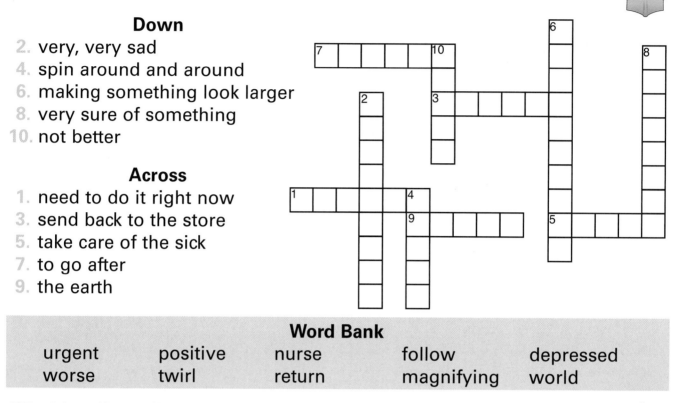

Word Bank				
urgent	positive	nurse	follow	depressed
worse	twirl	return	magnifying	world

Inventions.

The telephone was invented in 1876; the first widely sold lightbulb was invented in 1879. The handheld camera was invented in 1888, and the tractor in 1900. What would you like to invent that could be important to you and others? Think of something you might invent in the future. Either write about or draw a picture of your invention, or both.

Use the graph to answer the questions.

Ms. Fran has many friends. She sends them letters each week. Mark the number of letters she sends each day **on the graph**. (Monday is done for you.) Then answer the questions. Each letter shown stands for four letters.

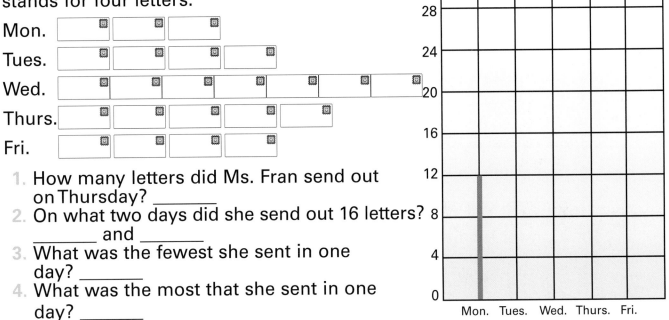

Mon.

Tues.

Wed.

Thurs.

Fri.

1. How many letters did Ms. Fran send out on Thursday? _____
2. On what two days did she send out 16 letters? _____ and _____
3. What was the fewest she sent in one day? _____
4. What was the most that she sent in one day? _____

Similarities and Differences. Look at each pair of words. Write down at least one way they are alike and at least one way they are different.

1. leopard and cheetah _____

_____

_____

2. typewriter and piano _____

_____

_____

3. cabin and tent _____

_____

_____

4. whistle and sing _____

_____

_____

Real or Make-Believe. Write M for make-believe or R for real.

_____ 1. a pumpkin growing on a vine in a field

_____ 2. a fireman saving a kitten from a tree

_____ 3. an elephant that can fly in a circus

_____ 4. a cow that can give chocolate milk

_____ 5. a family taking a summer vacation

_____ 6. a chicken that lays golden eggs

_____ 7. a brother and sister working together

_____ 8. five children going to a movie in the afternoon

_____ 9. buckets of paint turning the sky many colors

_____ 10. a ghost turning a frog into a king

_____ 11. a tree being blown over by the wind

_____ 12. a rainbow bridge to the moon

Use the clue to help you fill in the missing letters. Hint: Use vowels.

1. to do something many times   __ft__n

2. a sea animal with eight legs   __ct__p__s

3. a reptile that lives in a swamp   cr__c__d__l__

4. a very small house   c__tt__ge

5. something to keep the rain off   __mbr__ll__

6. twelve things   d__z__n

7. a tree or the inner part of your hand   p__lm

8. two things that are different   __pp__s__t__

9. a place that has little rain   d__s__rt

10. you can put this on a Christmas tree   __rn__m__nt

11. a dessert made with eggs   c__st__rd

12. to stop something from happening   pr__v__nt

13. go away   d__s__pp__ __r

14. to say you are sorry   __p__l__g__z__

Perimeter is the measurement of the length around a figure. You can find the perimeter by adding the lengths of all the sides. Look at the following figures and find the perimeter of each.

1.

2

2   2

2

perimeter = _____ units

2.

4

2   2

4

perimeter = _____ units

Which two words make up each contraction, or what contraction comes from the two words?

1. Write the contractions for these words.

   we are   _____   was not   _____

   were not   _____   would not   _____

2. Write the two words in these contractions.

   they've   _____   shouldn't   _____

   they'll   _____   I'd   _____

3. Write the contractions for these words.

   he is   _____   she is   _____

   he has   _____   she has   _____

4. Write the contractions for these words.

   let us   _____   will not   _____

   does not   _____   we have   _____

Read the directions in the box. Draw a line under the answer to each question.

1. What do the directions tell you how to make?
   a. oatmeal
   b. instant oatmeal
   c. cold cereal

Instant Oatmeal
1. Empty package into microwaveable bowl.
2. Add 2/3 cup water or milk and stir.
3. Microwave on high 1–2 minutes; stir.
4. Put milk and sugar on top.
5. Eat with a spoon.
6. Clean up.

---

2. What is the first step?
   a. turn microwave on
   b. empty package into bowl
   c. stir well to mix

3. What things do you need?
   oatmeal package, pan, water or milk, spoon, flour, sugar

4. How long should it take you to make this?
   a. a few seconds   b. a few minutes   c. 30 minutes

Add a prefix to the word after the blank. Use re- or un-.

1. Please _____move your shoes before you come in.

2. We will have to _____build our house.

3. He was very _____kind to me.

4. I would like to _____ join that club.

5. That was an _____usual movie.

6. We have to _____make the cake.

7. Did you feel like you were treated _____fairly?

8. The children will _____turn on Saturday.

9. That was an _____common rainstorm.

10. You will have to _____wrap that gift.

Practice finding the differences.

EX.

5 10	300	510	804	905	404
6̸Ø3	− 130	− 250	− 163	− 662	− 142
− 240					
363					

EX.

4 9 10	623	771	900	435	500
5̸ØØ	− 257	− 704	− 156	− 297	− 297
− 246					
254					

EX.

8 14 10	$5.00	$6.15	$10.32	$4.06	$1.00
$9̸.5̸Ø	− 1.62	− 4.38	− 7.75	− 1.67	− .67
− 6.75					
$2.75					

Write, in cursive, a sentence for each of the -es words in the box.

hooves

lives

leaves

scarves

wives

wolves

1. _____

_____

2. _____

_____

3. _____

_____

4. _____

_____

5. _____

_____

6. _____

_____

Look at this table of contents and answer the questions.

1. What chapters should you read to learn how to write a story?

   _____, _____

2. On what page should you start reading to learn about commas?

   _____

3. How many chapters does this table of contents show? _____

4. On which page would you find information on describing what something looks like? _____

5. Which chapter might tell you how to make a paper airplane? _____

   _____

FACTOID
Most insects must turn their whole bodies to turn their heads—but the praying mantis doesn't need to.

Table of Contents

Read the paragraph and add the correct punctuation.

Where did you go yesterday Tanner asked Denise I went to the fair she told him I will draw a picture of it for you She then told him about the watermelon-eating contest and the blue ribbon she won She told him about seeing pigs and prize-winning sheep It sounds like you had a fun day Denise I wish I had been with you said Tanner.

Now draw a picture of something else Denise may have seen at the fair.

Read and solve the problems.

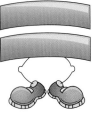

1. James planted 5 corn seeds each in 9 holes. How many seeds did he plant?

_____ x _____ = _____

2. Judy went to a book sale. In 3 days, she bought 24 books. She bought the same number each time she went. How many did she buy each day? _____

3. Betty has the same number of nickels as she has dimes. She has $1.80 worth of dimes. How many nickels does she have? _____ She has $ ____.____ in nickels.

4. Sue babysat four times last week. She made $4 one night, $5.25 on two different nights, and $6.40 on one night. How much did Sue make altogether? _____

5. There were 95 children on the bus. Ten got off at the first stop. Twenty-two got off at the second stop. How many are left on the bus? _____

6. Allen picked fruit for a farmer last summer. He picked 16 bushels of peaches, 14 bushels of apples, and 18 bushels of pears. How much fruit did Allen pick? _____

Write the titles of these books correctly. <u>Remember</u>: the first, last, and all important words need to begin with a capital letter. Write in cursive.

1. nate the great _____

2. katy and the big snow _____

3. claude the dog _____

4. emma's dragon hunt _____

5. the legend of the bluebonnet _____

6. the seashore story _____

7. soup for the king _____

8. the storm book _____

Finish writing this story.

The group of hikers did not know how long it had been since anyone had seen Don. "I know he was here just a little while ago," said Fred. Fred had said that two hours ago. There were already search parties out looking for Don.

"Don is a good hiker and should be able to find his way down the mountain," his father was saying. "But maybe he has been hurt," replied Don's friend, Craig.

_____

_____

_____

_____

_____

_____

_____

Try making a comparison with nature or something else.

EXAMPLE: The first daffodils were as yellow as _lemons_ .

1. The piano keys were as white as _____.

2. That horse is as black as a dark _____.

3. The fireworks were as bright as the _____.

4. Her eyes were as green as the _____.

5. That house was as tall as a steep _____.

6. The balloons reminded me of a bunch of _____.

7. The mud between my toes was as brown as _____.

8. The sunset was as red and orange as _____.

9. The rings on her fingers sparkled like _____.

10. The wind was as gentle as _____.

11. The new leaves on the trees in spring are as green as_____.

12. My new sweater was as blue as the summer _____.

Count the money.

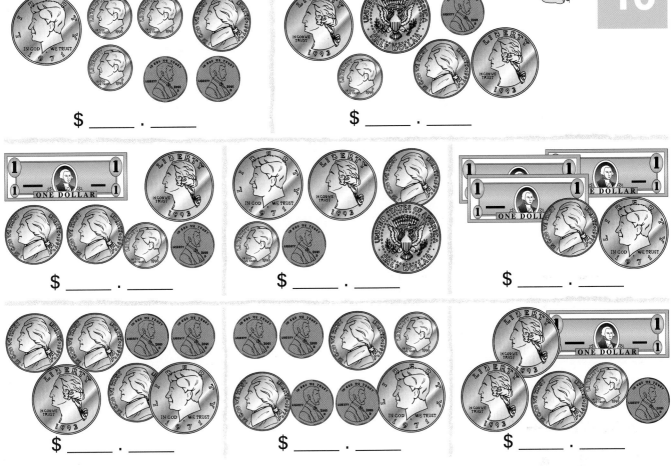

$ _____ . _____

$ _____ . _____

$ _____ . _____

$ _____ . _____

$ _____ . _____

$ _____ . _____

$ _____ . _____

$ _____ . _____

The <u>main idea</u> tells what a story is all about. Usually, one sentence tells the main idea. Find the sentence in the story that tells the main idea and underline it.

1. Penny Puppy eats strange snacks. She likes to chew on old socks, making holes in them. She eats pussy willows and catnip leaves. Her favorite snack is bug bars. However, whenever you see Penny Puppy, she will always have a snack bone necklace around her neck.

2. Oliver Owl tries to teach Ollie Owl how to fly, but Ollie has a difficult time learning. Oliver tells Ollie to perch on the highest branch of the tallest tree. "Then jump and flap your little wings as hard as you can!" he says. Ollie tries but just somersaults all the way down. Oliver just barely catches Ollie on the last branch. Oliver decides he was not meant to teach little owls how to fly!

Write a story about the picture. Be sure to use capital letters and periods where needed. Give your story a title.

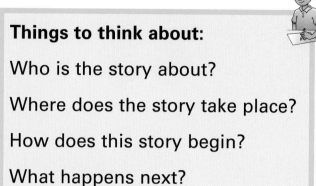

Things to think about:

Who is the story about?

Where does the story take place?

How does this story begin?

What happens next?

How will this story end?

Use the information given on meters and kilometers to help you solve the problems.

1 meter = 100 centimeters   1 kilometer = 1,000 meters
cm = centimeter   m = meter   km = kilometer

Choose a unit so the answers seem reasonable.

1. Randy is 150 _____ tall.

2. Jane's room is 5 _____ wide.

3. Whitney's hand is 14 _____ long and 5 _____ wide.

4. The distance from Florida to Texas is 1,150 _____.

5. The flagpole at the post office is 46 _____ tall.

6. I can touch the wall 163 _____ high.

7. Mr. Hobbs drove his car 84 _____ the first hour.

8. Joyce's room is about 6 _____ wide.

9. Jack and Jill walked approximately 3 _____ in 30 minutes.

Writers sometimes use words that stand for other words. They call them <u>word referents</u>. Read each sentence. Circle the word that the underlined word stands for.

EXAMPLE:

1. Betty has a (computer) She keeps <u>it</u> on her desk.

2. Dora said, "I have to go home now to visit <u>my</u> grandmother."

3. Bill asked Juan if <u>he</u> was going to play baseball this year.

4. Jack and Jean both collect seashells. Sometimes <u>they</u> trade with one another.

5. Rachel plays the violin, and sometimes <u>she</u> sings, too.

6. When the big, gray dog saw the cat, <u>it</u> barked and growled.

7. Our school bus is always crowded, and <u>it</u> is usually very noisy, too.

8. Mom might let us go sledding today. We might get <u>her</u> to drive us to the hill at the park.

Read the story and answer the questions.

Denise has a dog named Pocket. Pocket hates to take a bath. Whenever he hears water running, Pocket runs outside and hides in the playhouse. Last week, Denise decided Pocket had to have a bath. Denise took a round tub out on the lawn and started to fill it with warm water. When the tub was ready, Denise called her dog. "Come here, Pocket. It's time for your bath."

1. Do you think Pocket will come to Denise? Why or why not?

_____

_____

2. Where do you think Denise will find Pocket? Why?

_____

_____

3. What would you do if you had a dog like Pocket?

_____

_____

Read the paragraph and answer the questions.

The children were playing baseball in the empty lot. Peggy was at bat. She swung hard and hit the ball farther than anyone else had. The ball sailed across the lot and smashed through Mrs. Allen's window. Peggy knew Mrs. Allen would be really angry. The other kids scattered, running for home. Peggy looked at the broken window.

1. What do you think Peggy will do?

_____

_____

_____

2. Which clues helped you to decide?

_____

_____

_____

Find the missing factors. One factor and the product are given to you.

1. ____ x 3 = 6	____ x 6 = 30	4 x ____ =16
2. 3 x ____ = 18	7 x ____ = 14	____ x 9 = 18
3. ____ x 5 = 5	12 x ____ = 12	____ x 8 = 24
4. 1 x ____ = 9	4 x ____ = 28	9 x ____ = 81
5. 3 x ____ = 21	____ x 5 = 25	____ x 7 = 49
6. ____ x 2 = 4	9 x ____ = 36	8 x ____ = 72
7. 5 x ____ = 45	2 x ____ = 30	10 x ____ = 50
8. 12 x ____ = 36	3 x ____ = 27	6 x ____ = 60

The words in each row go together in some way. Write two more words to go with them.

EXAMPLE:

1. robin, owl, pigeon ___*quail*___ ___*pheasant*___
2. peaches, apples, pears _____ _____
3. spoon, bowl, cup _____ _____
4. lake, pond, river _____ _____
5. branch, sticks, wood _____ _____
6. lemonade, water, milk _____ _____
7. dollar, dime, penny _____ _____
8. carrot, celery, pears _____ _____
9. dress, shoes, skirt _____ _____
10. tennis, golf, racquetball _____ _____

Fill in the blanks using these words: <u>plant</u>, <u>heat</u>, <u>sunlight</u>, <u>plants</u>, <u>Earth</u>, <u>sunlight</u>, <u>oxygen</u>. **Then answer the questions below.**

Sunlight is very important to our planet, _____. It provides us with food, oxygen, and _____. Most of our food comes from _____ life. _____ also give off the _____ we breathe. Without _____, plants would die, and we would not have food or air. The _____ also heats the earth. Without it, we would freeze to death.

1. What is the topic?

   a. food

   b. sunlight

   c. oxygen

   d. plants

2. What is the main idea?

   a. Sunlight is important to the earth.

   b. Sunlight heats plants.

   c. People would freeze without sunlight.

   d. Sunlight hurts your eyes.

Words that mean about the same thing are called <u>synonyms</u>. Write, in cursive, a synonym from the box below for the word listed.

EX. **easy** _simple_	shout	change
also	jacket	home
gift	car	complete
close	gem	join
shy	penny	mistake
wet	rug	argument
rich	couch	scared

~~simple~~	yell	present	timid	house	shut	afraid
finish	jewel	sofa	coat	error	automobile	moist
too	carpet	wealthy	alter	cent	connect	dispute

Mixed Skill Practice.

12	8	6	15	6	13	14
− 8	+ 9	x 4	− 9	x 7	− 5	+ 7

19	46	75	38	44	83	57
+ 39	− 28	− 39	+ 17	− 15	− 47	+ 34

8	4	3	27	40	35	65
x 4	x 7	x 9	+ 19	− 8	+ 44	− 59

804	132	176	921	608	304	657
− 238	− 78	+ 394	+ 496	− 239	− 127	− 589

Pretend you were walking in a park last night and saw a spaceship land. Write a paragraph about it. How did it look? How did it make you feel? Did anyone else see it? Did you see or speak to anyone or anything?

www.SummerBridgeActivities.com
73
© Summer Bridge Activities™ 3–4

Divide the shapes according to the fraction asked for.

EXAMPLE:

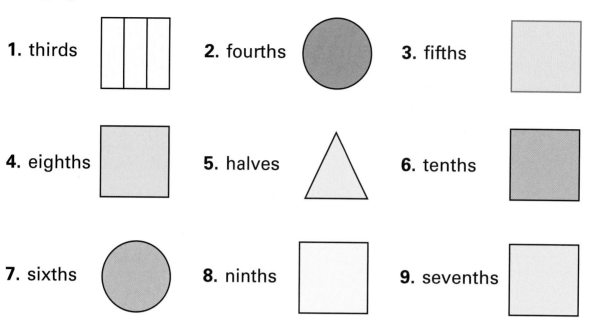

1. thirds

2. fourths

3. fifths

4. eighths

5. halves

6. tenths

7. sixths

8. ninths

9. sevenths

10. Start with a paper strip ⬚⬚⬚⬚. Fold it once. Fold it again. Fold it once more. Before you unfold it, think to yourself, "How do the folds divide the paper, and how many equal parts do I have?" Now check to see if you are right.

Write the words under the correct word category.

buttermilk
airplane
snowstorm
selection
replanted
overweight
sleepless
peaceful
happiness
football
daylight
unpacked

Compound words	Words with prefixes or suffixes

Read the story carefully. Watch for word meanings.

Matt lives in a large city with his grandparents. The building that he and his grandparents live in is very tall and has different sets of rooms for each family that lives there. This building is called an apartment. In this neighborhood, all of the buildings are fairly tall and close together. People do not have to go far to get things in this urban area. Matt's cousin, Damon, lives in a small, rural, country community. He has a large backyard to play in instead of a park like Matt. There is a lot of space between the houses where Damon lives. Both Matt's and Damon's neighborhoods have schools, hospitals, stores, and other places people need.

Write down a meaning for each of the following words:

1. community _____

_____

2. apartment _____

_____

3. rural area _____

Write a short paragraph about your home and community.

It's Time Again!

1. Write the times.

____:____   ____:____   ____:____   ____:____

2. Look at the clock below and answer the questions.

What time does the clock show? _____

What time would it have been 15 minutes earlier? _____

What time will it be in half an hour? _____

Can you think of a way to write the time
other than the way you wrote it before? _____

What time would it show if you switched the hands? _____

Find the correctly spelled word. Circle it; then write it in the blank to complete the sentence.

1. Astronauts are _____ while they are out in space.

   waitless   **weightless**   **waghtless**   **wateless**

2. The _____ children picked up litter along the streets.

   thotful   **toughtful**   **thoughtful**   **thowghtful**

3. The _____ woman invited the new family for dinner.

   neighborly   **neighborlie**   **naborly**   **knaborly**

4. We need to remember to keep our doctor's _____.

   apointment   **apowntment**   **appointment**

5. Make some _____ of this, please.

   copyes   **copies**   **copeis**   **coppies**

Jet

This is one of those planes that your mother always warned you to be careful with because it could poke someone's eye out. Find a large, open area and throw it as hard as you can.

Stuff You Need:

paper (8 ½" x 11")

Here's What to Do:

1. Fold the paper in half vertically, and then unfold it.

2. Grab one top corner and fold it down to the middle fold. Do the same thing for the other side. You should now have something that looks like the outline of a house.

3. Grab the new edges and fold them over into the middle one more time. You now have a very steep A-frame house.

4. Fold the airplane in half so that the folds are in the inside.

5. The last fold is for the wings. Fold each side of the airplane down, starting from the tip and folding so that the edge of the wing matches up perfectly with the bottom of the plane. If you want to make the plane even stronger, tape the wings together.

6. Your completed airplane should look like the illustration. Now all you have to do is take your airplane outside and let it soar!

1.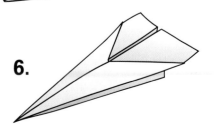

2.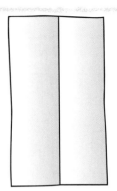

3.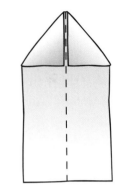

4.

5.

6.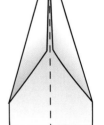

Instant Rock

You probably pick up rocks every now and then without thinking about how it takes a very long time for them to form. To start learning about rocks, make a few of your own!

Stuff You Need:

| plastic bowl | milk carton (1-pint) | sand |
| spoon | water | white glue |

Here's What to Do:

1. Mix one part water and two parts white glue in a plastic bowl. Stir the goop well.

2. Clean an empty milk carton. Fill it with sand. Leave about half an inch of space at the top.

3. Pour the glue-and-water mixture into the carton until it comes just to the top of the sand. Let it harden for one full day. (Two days would be better if you live in a humid climate.)

4. After the mixture has hardened, peel the carton away from the sand. You can use your newly formed rock as a paper weight or garden ornament.

What's This All About?

Some kinds of rocks form over long periods of time. Wind and water leave sand, silt, and dead plant and animal matter in layers. The dead things turn to fossils if they are buried quickly enough. As time passes, the layers get deeper and deeper. As you can imagine, the weight of all of this muck smooshes the sand at the bottom. It is held together like cement to make a sedimentary rock, or rock made of sediment (smooshed silt and sand). The different colors in the rock are caused by different kinds of minerals and ores. Red is usually iron, blue is copper, black is manganese, and so on.

More Fun Ideas to Try:

1. You may want to make "rocks" using other things besides glue. Try adding water to flour, cornstarch, sugar, and baking soda. Once you have done that, try using different materials in place of the sand. Try to break some of your rocks. Which materials make the hardest rock?

2. Sedimentary rocks abound in formations throughout the United States. A trip to a local museum of natural history may be in order. Or, if there is a rock shop in the area, go and view its collection.

3. For the ultimate in sedimentary rock formations, study or visit the Grand Circle in Utah, Arizona, New Mexico, and Colorado.

Motivational Calendar

Month

My parents and I decided that if I complete
15 days of **Summer Bridge Activities**™ and
read _____ minutes a day, my incentive/reward will be:

Child's Signature _____ Parent's Signature_____

Day 1	☆	📖	_____	**Day 9**	☆	📖	_____
Day 2	☆	📖	_____	**Day 10**	☆	📖	_____
Day 3	☆	📖	_____	**Day 11**	☆	📖	_____
Day 4	☆	📖	_____	**Day 12**	☆	📖	_____
Day 5	☆	📖	_____	**Day 13**	☆	📖	_____
Day 6	☆	📖	_____	**Day 14**	☆	📖	_____
Day 7	☆	📖	_____	**Day 15**	☆	📖	_____
Day 8	☆	📖	_____				

Child: Color the ☆ for daily activities completed.
Color the 📖 for daily reading completed.

Parent: Initial the ____ when all activities are complete.

Discover Something New!

Fun Activity Ideas to Go Along with the Third Section!

1. Put on a play using old clothes as costumes.

2. Make a game of practicing times tables.

3. Use a block of ice to cool off and slide down a grassy hill.

4. Make snow cones with crushed ice and Kool-Aid.

5. Surprise an elderly neighbor by weeding his/her garden.

6. Create a family symphony with bottles, pans, and rubber bands.

7. Write a letter to a relative.

8. Browse for school clothes. Calculate the money needed for purchases.

9. Go to the woods or lake for an early morning "bird watch."

10. Finger-paint—outside.

11. Lie on the grass and pick designs out of the clouds.

12. Read some library books about birds.

13. Make some 3-D art using feathers, twigs, etc.

14. Paint the sidewalk with water.

15. Collect sticks and mud—then build a bird's nest.

Counting Change.

Spent	Gave clerk	How much change?
EXAMPLE: $1.35	$1.50	$.15
$2.50	$5.00	
$.95	$1.00	
$1.80	$2.00	
$6.42	$10.00	

Spent	Gave clerk	How much change?
$9.35	$20.00	
$5.55	$6.00	
$13.95	$20.00	
$85.00	$100.00	
$100.60	$105.00	

Have you seen a parade this summer? If so, write about it. If not, make up a story about a circus parade. Give it a title. Write in cursive.

_____

_____

_____

_____

_____

_____

_____

_____

_____

_____

_____

Look at the first word in each row; then find the words in the row that have the same vowel sound. Circle them. (Hint: They do not need to have the same vowels.)

1. noise — joy   choose   choice   boy   mower   voice

2. wrote — frog   both   coat   know   bought   grow

3. book — choose   look   foot   spoon   tooth   hook

4. there — bear   hair   share   near   bread   spare

5. large — star   yard   scare   mark   guard   far

6. proud — slow   crowd   now   ouch   shout   round

7. taste — eight   white   wait   height   paint   ate

8. work — world   store   short   word   stork   fourth

The "stressed" syllable is said with a little more force than the others. Circle the stressed syllable in each of the following words. Use a dictionary if you need help. In a dictionary, the stressed syllable is preceded or followed by an accent mark (').

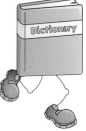

EXAMPLE:

1. es cape′   es (cape)
2. de tec tive
3. doc tor
4. com plete
5. mes sen ger
6. mead ow
7. gar den
8. man age
9. un til
10. sur prise
11. re sult
12. con tain er
13. li ons
14. daugh ter
15. es ca la tor
16. fac to ry
17. char ac ter
18. at ten tion

Multiplication and division facts are related.

6 x 3 = 18   3 x 6 = 18   18 ÷ 6 = 3   18 ÷ 3 = 6

Use what you know to write the related facts for each problem.

1. 5 x 3 = ____
____ x ____ = ____
____ ÷ ____ = ____
____ ÷ ____ = ____

2. 7 x 3 = ____
____ x ____ = ____
____ ÷ ____ = ____
____ ÷ ____ = ____

3. 6 x 4 = ____
____ x ____ = ____
____ ÷ ____ = ____
____ ÷ ____ = ____

4. 5 x 6 = ____
____ x ____ = ____
____ ÷ ____ = ____
____ ÷ ____ = ____

5. 9 x 2 = ____
____ x ____ = ____
____ ÷ ____ = ____
____ ÷ ____ = ____

6. 4 x 3 = ____
____ x ____ = ____
____ ÷ ____ = ____
____ ÷ ____ = ____

7. 4 x 8 = ____
____ x ____ = ____
____ ÷ ____ = ____
____ ÷ ____ = ____

8. 9 x 4 = ____
____ x ____ = ____
____ ÷ ____ = ____
____ ÷ ____ = ____

Make up one of your own.

____ x ____ = ____   ____ ÷ ____ = ____

____ x ____ = ____   ____ ÷ ____ = ____

Find the probability.

Penny has 11 pencils in her pencil box. Two pencils are orange, 3 pencils are blue, 5 pencils are yellow, and 1 pencil is green.

1. What is the probability that Penny will pull out an **orange** pencil?

   2 out of 11, or $\frac{2}{11}$

2. What is the probability that Penny will pull out a **black** pencil?

3. What is the probability that Penny will pull out a **green** pencil?

4. What is the probability that Penny will pull out a **yellow** pencil?

5. What is the probability that Penny will pull out a **blue** pencil?

6. What color pencil is Penny **most likely** to pull out of her pencil box?

Choose the correct meaning for each word.

____ stick   **1.** the very middle

____ choice   **2.** upward movement

____ nickel   **3.** to catch and hold

____ neat   **4.** thin piece of wood

____ pretend   **5.** use foolishly

____ waste   **6.** floor covering

____ center   **7.** right to choose

____ trap   **8.** a coin

____ spring   **9.** small break

____ crack   **10.** large bird

____ quiet   **11.** make-believe

____ stork   **12.** people who live near

____ neighbors   **13.** good order

____ rug   **14.** very little noise

Now write your own meaning for these words:

1. shine
_____

2. dream
_____

3 different
_____

4. bored
_____

5. weird
_____

Number these sentences in the correct order.

____ Off to the moon went Joan!

____ Joan found an old tuna can.

____ Joan told the strange animal she wanted a trip to the moon.

____ She washed the tuna can in the creek.

____ The animal said it would send her to the moon if she gave it a pair of pink rollerblades.

____ A strange animal appeared and told her she could have a wish.

____ Joan got the rollerblades and gave them to the strange animal.

Draw the strange animal.

Division: There are two ways of writing it.

1. $18 \div 3 =$ _____

2. $24 \div 4 =$ _____

3. $10 \div 2 =$ _____

4. $21 \div 3 =$ _____

5. $36 \div 4 =$ _____

6. $32 \div 8 =$ _____

7. $18 \div 3 =$ _____

8. $45 \div 5 =$ _____

9. $48 \div 6 =$ _____

10. $42 \div 7 =$ _____

11. $5\overline{)40}$

12. $9\overline{)36}$

13. $4\overline{)12}$

14. $7\overline{)56}$

15. $4\overline{)16}$

16. $6\overline{)36}$

17. $8\overline{)40}$

18. $9\overline{)27}$

19. $6\overline{)42}$

20. $7\overline{)35}$

Some verbs show present tense, some show past tense, and some need a helping verb. Examples: <u>go</u>, <u>give</u>, <u>take</u> = present; <u>did</u>, <u>went</u>, <u>ran</u> = past; <u>done</u> and <u>gone</u> need helpers. Underline the verb and then write if it is present, past, or has a helper.

EXAMPLE:

1. Mom <u>was</u> in a good mood.   _past_

2. I broke my mother's favorite vase yesterday. _____

3. Mr. Peep has given that talk many times. _____

4. I run down the hill every day. _____

5. Her mom can take us to the ball game. _____

6. Jane did the dishes by herself. _____

7. You have gone to this school for five years. _____

8. Please give me the money now. _____

Batter Up, Batter Up.

FACTOID
Did you know that the dot on top of the letter "i" has a name? It's called a tittle.

J. J. stepped up to the plate and waited for the pitcher to throw the ball. The pitcher pitched the ball too high, but J. J. swung at it anyway. The next ball was pitched right down the center. It was so fast, J. J. missed it completely. It was not his day. The other team's fans hooted when the pitcher struck him out. He felt bad. His feelings were hurt because some people laughed at him. He also felt he had let his teammates down. He was not a quitter, though.

Write down what you think happened or should happen next with J. J. and his team.

_____

_____

_____

_____

_____

Read the words in each group. List what you think comes first, second, and third.

____ time school's out
____ summertime is the
____ and vacations begin

____ and get tan in the sun
____ the sprinklers
____ let's run through

____ for Father's Day
____ and sunshine
____ June is the time

____ Independence Day is
____ always, always on the
____ fourth of July

____ Little Lost River
____ my family always
____ goes fishing on

____ ice cream are summer foods
____ baked beans, and
____ hot dogs, potato chips,

Area is the space inside a figure. It is measured in square units. You can find the area by adding the number of squares in the figure. Look at the following figures and find the area of each.

1.

2.

area = _____square units

area = _____square units

Do you remember the parts of a friendly letter?

Label the parts of this letter:

Body

Closing

Greeting

Signature

Heading _____

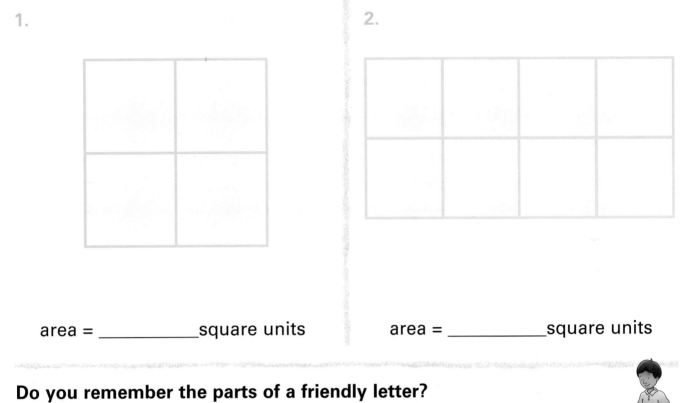

1921 King Street
Boise, Idaho
August 2, 2006

_____

Dear Sara, _____

    I am having a great time at camp. I swim every day and hike a lot, too. Yesterday, our group hiked five miles.

I hope you are feeling better.

_____   Your friend,

_____   Bugs

Cause and Effect. Read the sentences; then circle the (effect,) the part that tells what happened. Underline the _cause_, the part that tells why it happened.

EXAMPLE: The sky became cloudy, (and then it started to snow.)

1. The cold weather caused frost to cover the windows.

2. The falling snowflakes made my cheeks wet and cold.

3. Snow stuck to my mittens because I had made a snowman.

4. The snowman melted from the heat of the sun.

5. I played so long in the sun, I got a bad sunburn.

6. Pinnochio's nose grew longer every time he told a lie.

7. Snow White woke up when the prince kissed her.

8. The lady went to the well to get a bucket of water.

9. Our big oak tree was blown down by a strong wind.

10. Miss Mouse got very fat because she ate so much cheese.

Pretend this island is out in the ocean. Answer the questions about it.

1. Which river runs into Lake Ho? _____

2. Which ocean is south of the island? _____

3. How many mountain ranges are there? _____

4. Which river is the longest? _____

5. What ocean is north of Pint Island? _____

6. What is the name of the capital city? _____

7. What direction is Hi Town from Toe Town? _____

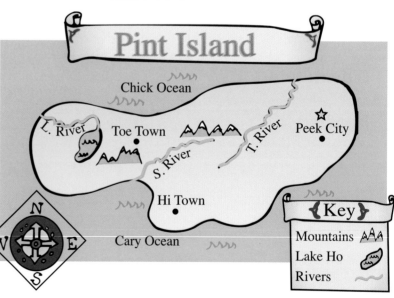

Division.

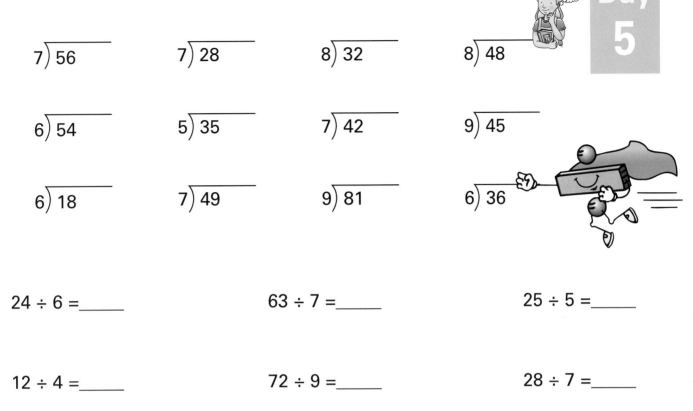

$7\overline{)56}$ $7\overline{)28}$ $8\overline{)32}$ $8\overline{)48}$

$6\overline{)54}$ $5\overline{)35}$ $7\overline{)42}$ $9\overline{)45}$

$6\overline{)18}$ $7\overline{)49}$ $9\overline{)81}$ $6\overline{)36}$

24 ÷ 6 = _____   63 ÷ 7 = _____   25 ÷ 5 = _____

12 ÷ 4 = _____   72 ÷ 9 = _____   28 ÷ 7 = _____

Circle the pronouns in the sentences. <u>Remember</u>: A pronoun takes the place of a noun. There can be more than one in some sentences.

1. I told her about Val's horse.
2. This piece of cake is for him.
3. Liz invited Joe and me to the party.
4. The table is all set for us.
5. We are too late to see the first show.
6. They will be happy to come with us.
7. Ray caught two bugs, and later he freed them.
8. This pie is for you and me to eat for dessert.
9. Lisa had a hard time doing the test, but it is over now.
10. Clams and turtles have shells. They are protected by them.
11. He is Jan's best friend.
12. They have been best friends for a long time.

Unscramble the words and write them correctly to complete the sentences.

1. <u>Pillows</u> are to <u>soft</u> as <u>boards</u> are to _____. **rdha**

2. <u>Oranges</u> are to <u>juicy</u> as <u>crackers</u> are to _____. **dyr**

3. <u>Braces</u> are to <u>teeth</u> as <u>glasses</u> are to _____. **esey**

4. <u>Bells</u> are to <u>ring</u> as <u>cars</u> are to _____. **nkho**

5. <u>Hear</u> is to <u>ears</u> as <u>touch</u> is to _____. **serinfg**

6. <u>Shout</u> is to <u>noise</u> as <u>whisper</u> is to _____. **uetqi**

7. <u>Star</u> is to <u>pointed</u> as <u>circle</u> is to _____. **dunor**

8. <u>Scaly</u> is to <u>fish</u> as <u>furry</u> is to _____. **ttnike**

9. <u>Ant</u> is to <u>crawl</u> as <u>frog</u> is to _____. **pael**

10. <u>Elephant</u> is to <u>large</u> as <u>mouse</u> is to _____. **malsl**

11. <u>Paint</u> is to <u>brush</u> as <u>draw</u> is to _____. **cienlp**

12. <u>Buckle</u> is to <u>belt</u> as <u>tie</u> is to _____. **laceheos**

Think of a story to fit the pictures. Write in the words.

Adding more than two addends.

65	22	78	51	42	87
59	46	32	26	39	32
+ 11	+ 38	+ 21	+ 26	+ 71	+ 19

54	38	39	43	37	17
19	22	71	36	46	19
+ 68	+ 46	+ 42	+ 18	+ 28	+ 12

215	325	429	742	395
463	48	330	135	205
+ 306	+ 113	+ 127	+ 173	+ 341

Read the following words. Write down how many vowels are in each word, how many vowel sounds you hear, and how many syllables there are.

		Number of vowels	Number of vowel sounds	Number of syllables
EXAMPLE:	**afraid**	3	2	2

	v	vs	syl
1. afternoon			
2. formula			
3. separated			
4. fantastic			
5. memories			
6. experience			
7. successful			

	v	vs	syl
8. education			
9. problem			
10. migrate			
11. submarine			
12. belated			
13. advertising			
14. characteristic			

Write your own ending for each sentence. Try to use more than two or three words. Write in cursive.

1. I like the flavor of_____.

2. My parents disapproved when I _____.

3. I once read a story about a boy who became
   a knight because he _____.

4. The rodeo started with_____.

5. Richard swam over to the dock to_____.

6. The kite drifted away _____.

7. The baby crawled across_____.

8. The long winter was beginning_____.

9. Lance won a prize for _____.

10. Do you like to play _____?

Can you put these puzzle pieces together and read the message? Don't cut them out. If you need more help, trace the pieces and practice on a sheet of scratch paper. The c and the m are already there to help you.

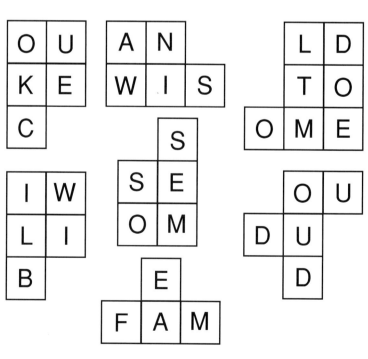

Find the products.

EXAMPLE:

```
  2
 58        42        67        66        35        23
x 3       x 8       x 5       x 3       x 6       x 3
---
174
```

```
 23        29        25        44        94        35
x 9       x 4       x 9       x 6       x 2       x 8
```

```
 25        21        75        68        41        63
x 4       x 6       x 4       x 3       x 7       x 2
```

A pronoun showing ownership is a <u>possessive</u> <u>pronoun</u>, such as…

| mine | ours | your | his | hers | their | its | my | our |

Write six sentences in cursive. Use a possessive pronoun in each one of them.

What does the underlined phrase really mean?
Circle your answer.

1. It was raining <u>cats and dogs</u>.
    a. Real cats and dogs were falling out of the sky.
    b. It was raining very hard.
    c. It wasn't raining at all.

2. The night was <u>black as coal</u>.
    a. The night was very dark.
    b. The sky was light.
    c. The night was turning into day.

3. I was so thirsty I felt like I <u>could spit cotton</u>.
    a. My mouth was very dry.
    b. I had cotton in my mouth.
    c. I did not need a drink.

4. The sun on the snow made it <u>sparkle like diamonds</u>.
    a. There were diamonds in the snow.
    b. The snow was dirty and dull.
    c. The snow was clean and shiny.

5. <u>Time flies</u> when we are having fun.
    a. Time goes quickly.
    b. Time has wings and flies like a bird.
    c. Time goes slowly.

6. The train <u>roared like a lion</u> as it went through the mountain pass.
    a. The train was quiet.
    b. The train has a voice.
    c. The train was loud and fast.

7. My sister is as <u>gentle as a lamb</u> with sick people.
    a. My sister is soft.
    b. My sister doesn't like sick people.
    c. My sister is kind to sick people.

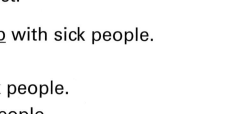

Find the quotients and the remainders.

EXAMPLE:

$$\overset{6\ R\ 2}{4\overline{)26}}$$ $3\overline{)14}$ $5\overline{)39}$ $3\overline{)16}$

$2\overline{)19}$ $6\overline{)29}$ $4\overline{)21}$ $5\overline{)36}$

$5\overline{)34}$ $4\overline{)22}$ $5\overline{)42}$ $4\overline{)33}$

$2\overline{)84}$ $3\overline{)60}$ $3\overline{)51}$ $4\overline{)96}$

Cursive writing review. School starts soon, so remember to…

1. Make each letter smooth and clear.
2. Space letters evenly.
3. Make each letter the correct shape and size.
4. Make each letter touch the line correctly.
5. Make your letters slant in the same direction.

Copy the following statement, or do one of your own!

I love to practice writing in cursive. It makes me feel very grown-up!

Get a dictionary. Look up the following words and write the special spelling for each word in the blank provided. Put in all the markings.

EXAMPLE:

magnolia mag nōl' y ə
<u>Remember</u>: **The special spelling tells you how to say a word correctly, how many syllables there are, where they are divided, and which syllable is stressed.**

1. porcupine _____   **2.** cupboard _____

3. electromagnet _____   **4.** chisel _____

5. elate _____   **6.** testify _____

7. gravity _____   **8.** nitrate _____

Choose three words from above and write their meanings.

1. word_____ meaning _____

2. word_____ meaning _____

3. word_____ meaning _____

We taste things because of our tongue and nose. The smell helps our tongue taste things. Ask your parents if you can taste some foods you have in your house. Tell whether they are bitter, sour, sweet, or salty. Write the name of the food you tasted under the correct heading.

EXAMPLE:

Bitter	Sour	Sweet	Salty
	lemon		

Complete the times table wheels.

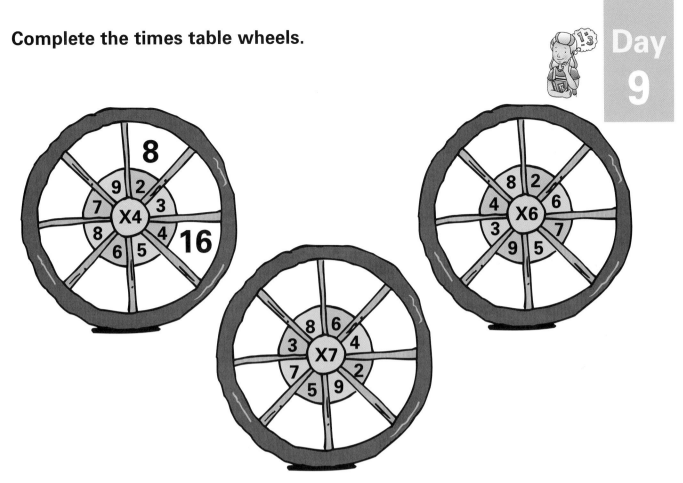

Underline the base, or root, word in each word.

blossoms	immediately	wreckage	incorrect
misspelled	inspector	retrace	reappear
exporting	invention	exhausted	messages

Underline the prefix in each word.

unusual	microphone	submarine	disappoint
displeased	invisible	extend	misplace
defrost	encircle	recover	enlarge

Underline the suffix in each word.

happiness	silently	tiniest	potatoes
hesitated	pleasantly	hasty	scarcely
mouthful	careless	graceful	spelling

Read each sentence. Put an <u>F</u> in the blank if the sentence is a fact. Write an <u>O</u> if it is an opinion. The first one has been done for you.

EXAMPLE:

1. Christmas is always on the 25th of December. _____<i>F</i>_____

2. Springtime is everyone's favorite time of year. _____

3. Birthdays are always a fun day for everyone. _____

4. Daylight and nighttime depend on the sun. _____

5. Dogs are said to be a man's best friend. _____

6. A spaceship travels faster than any airplane. _____

7. Lava rock was once a hot liquid. _____

8. Eating too much candy is hard on your teeth. _____

9. Most children like hot dogs and ice cream. _____

10. Reading is one of the most important things in our lives. _____

Making Comparisons. Cut an apple in half, draw a picture of it, and label the parts. Draw a picture of the earth. Pretend that you cut a section out. Label its parts.

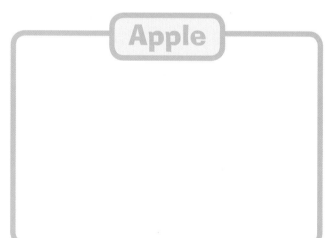

Apple

Earth

1. How is the apple similar to the inside of the earth?

_____

_____

2. How is the apple different from the inside of the earth?

_____

_____

Match the division and multiplication problems that are related.

EXAMPLE:

12 ÷ 4	5 x 5	38 ÷ 2	13 x 5
16 ÷ 8	3 x 4	63 ÷ 3	22 x 4
15 ÷ 5	9 x 4	50 ÷ 2	19 x 2
24 ÷ 6	6 x 4	84 ÷ 3	21 x 3
36 ÷ 9	9 x 5	56 ÷ 4	43 x 2
45 ÷ 5	3 x 5	86 ÷ 2	25 x 2
28 ÷ 7	7 x 4	88 ÷ 4	43 x 2
20 ÷ 4	2 x 8	65 ÷ 5	14 x 4
64 ÷ 8	5 x 4	80 ÷ 5	28 x 3
25 ÷ 5	8 x 8	72 ÷ 4	16 x 5
81 ÷ 9	8 x 9	51 ÷ 3	17 x 3
72 ÷ 9	9 x 9	86 ÷ 2	18 x 4

Look at the first word in each row. Circle the other words in the row that have the same vowel sound. Write a word of your own to go with the others with the same vowel sound.

1. team —	treat	chief	earth	sheep	_____
2. toast —	bowl	cow	both	though	_____
3. group —	truth	jump	cool	troop	_____
4. roll —	boat	stole	pool	told	_____
5. scoop —	droop	juice	soup	cook	_____
6. yawn —	jaws	chose	salt	lawn	_____
7. twice —	died	buy	since	price	_____
8. third —	church	torn	earth	fern	_____

Can you put the words in these mixed-up sentences in order to make sense?

1. flowers knows Jennifer to plant how

_____

- -

2. night could rainbows there at be

_____

- -

3. sky the into hot balloon up went air the

_____

- -

4. nobody new name knows the person's

_____

- -

_____

Answer the questions about the underlined word in each sentence. Use a dictionary if you need one.

1. He is a <u>skillful</u> artist.
    a. What is the suffix in the word?
    b. How would you divide the word into syllables? _____
    c. What is the base word? _____
2. A <u>harquebus</u> is an early type of firearm.
    a. How many syllables does the word have? _____
    b. Is it a compound word? _____
    c. What is the vowel sound in the last syllable? _____
3. I was <u>heartbroken</u> when my puppy was run over by a car.
    a. What are the two words in this compound word?
    _____ and _____
    b. How many syllables does it have? _____
    c. What is the base word for <u>broken</u>? _____
4. You acted in a <u>disorderly</u> manner.
    a. What does this word mean? _____
    b. Write it the special spelling way. _____
    c. What is the prefix in this word? _____
    d. What is the suffix? _____

Estimate. Circle the answer you think is best.

1. A bathtub would hold (10 quarts or 10 gallons) of water.

2. A flower vase would hold (1 pint or 1 gallon) of water.

3. A fishbowl would hold (3 quarts or 3 cups) of water.

4. A big glass would hold (1 pint or 1 quart) of milk.

5. A bicycle would weigh (20 ounces or 20 pounds).

6. An orange would weigh (7 ounces or 7 pounds).

7. A new pencil would weigh (1 ounce or 1 pound).

8. A cob of corn would be (11 inches or 11 yards) long.

9. A new pencil would be (7 inches or 7 yards) long.

10. A person could read a 1,500-page book in (16 minutes or 16 hours).

**Negative words are words with <u>no</u> or <u>not</u> in them.
Never use two <u>not</u>-words or <u>no</u>-words together.
Underline the correct answer.**

EXAMPLE:

| Don't be no litter bug. | wrong |
| Don't be a litter bug. | right |

1. There aren't (no, any) letters for you today.

2. I don't (ever, never) get to go camping.

3. Most snakes don't hurt (anybody, nobody).

4. Rob bumped his head; he doesn't remember (nothing, anything).

5. I (haven't, have) never flown in a jet.

6. I don't have (no, any) work left to do.

7. There is never (anything, nothing) fun to do on Saturday.

8. Can't (nobody, anybody) fix this step?

Read this story and answer the questions by drawing your own conclusions.

Julie Ann and Clint closed their eyes to shut out the sun's glare. As they lay on the ground, the hot July sun felt good. They could hear the wind blowing ever so softly through the pine trees, making a kind of whispering, murmuring sound. They could hear the creek nearby making soothing, babbling sounds. They could even hear the distant screech of a hawk flying high in the sky overhead.

1. Where do you think they are? _____

2. What season of the year is it? _____

3. What other creatures do you think could be there? _____

4. What would you like to do if you were there? _____

_____

Design a funny or clever birthday party invitation.

Find the sums.

246 + 129	500 + 806	924 + 289	402 + 629	550 + 758

1,284 + 2,629	7,762 + 1,473	3,383 + 5,007	4,290 + 2,968	4,006 + 6,974

9,542 + 695	2,423 + 1,932	3,252 + 4,008	6,666 + 4,208	1,920 + 1,940

An <u>adjective</u> is a word that describes a noun. Fill in the blanks with adjectives.

EXAMPLE:

1. The bathroom is _____**red**_____.

2. A _____ family moved in next door yesterday.

3. The bear has _____, _____ fur.

4. The _____ birds woke me up this morning.

5. Her _____, _____ balloon floated away.

Some adjectives tell which one. Use <u>this</u> and <u>that</u> with singular nouns, <u>these</u> and <u>those</u> with plural nouns.

1. _____ kittens are making too much noise.

2. _____ book is too long for me to read.

3. Is _____ one the hat Mom wanted?

4. _____ planet is very far away.

5. _____ ducks didn't come back to the pond this year.

Read the paragraph and answer the questions below.

   Ann and her brother took swimming lessons this summer. Because they lived in the country, they had to take a bus to the pool. It took a half hour to get there. Their lessons were two hours long, and then they had to ride the bus home. Even though it took a lot of time, they enjoyed it very much, and by the end of the summer, they both knew how to swim well.

Circle the letter of the best summary for this paragraph.

a. Ann and her brother took swimming lessons this summer.

b. Ann and her brother rode a bus to the pool to take swimming lessons this summer. They enjoyed it and both learned how to swim.

Answer these questions.

1. Should a summary be longer or shorter than the original paragraph?

_____

2. What information should be in the summary?

_____

It is almost time for school to start. You are going shopping for new school clothes. Draw and color some of the clothes and things you would like for school this year.

Solve these problems.

1. Don was picking apples. He put 36 apples in each box. How many apples did he put in 9 boxes?

_____

2. Miss Brown has 25 children in her class. She wants to make 5 equal teams for a relay race. How many children will be on each team?_____

3. Ted has saved $9.00 toward buying a new ball. He will get $3.00 today from his father. How much more will he need to buy the $19.95 ball?

_____

4. Judy saved 867 pennies in May, 942 in July, and 716 in June. How many pennies did she save in these three months? _____ How many more pennies did she save in July than June?_____

5. Lou needs 5 dozen eggs for a picnic. How many eggs does he need?

_____

6. Fred got a pie for his birthday. He ate 1/2 of the pie that day. He ate 1/4 of it the next day. How much did he have left?

_____

Use the before singular and plural nouns.
Use a or an before singular nouns only.
Use a before words beginning with consonant sounds.
Use an before words beginning with vowel sounds.

Fill in the blanks. Use a, the, or an.

1. _____ orange rolled out of my sock.

2. That spider is _____ useful creature.

3. _____ ice fell off the roof.

4. I love to watch _____ parrots when I go to _____ zoo.

5. Have you ever seen _____ octopus?

6. My mother lost _____ earring.

7. My brother, Ron, can play _____ drum.

8. _____ floor is covered with newspapers.

SUPER STAR

105

Where would you find the answers to the following questions? Write the name of the reference aid you would use on the line.

globe	dictionary	encyclopedia

1. Where is Utah? _____
2. How do they harvest sugar cane in Hawaii? _____
3. Which syllable is stressed in the word profit? _____
4. What kind of food do people eat in Mexico? _____
5. Which continent is closest to Australia? _____
6. Where is the Indian Ocean? _____
7. Who was Thomas Edison, and what did he do? _____
8. What does hibernate mean? _____
9. Where do you find guide words? _____
10. Was England involved in the Second World War? _____

Choose the correct spelling for each word. Fill in the circle.

EXAMPLE:
    ○ babys   ○ babeys   ● babies   ○ babby

1. ○ storys   ○ stories   ○ storyes   ○ storiees
2. ○ crid   ○ cryed   ○ cried   ○ kried
3. ○ seiling   ○ ceiling   ○ cieling   ○ sieling
4. ○ certain   ○ sertin   ○ cirtaen   ○ sertain
5. ○ citty   ○ citey   ○ sity   ○ city
6. ○ matr   ○ matter   ○ mator   ○ mater
7. ○ sound   ○ soun   ○ sownd   ○ sounde
8. ○ ucross   ○ acos   ○ ecross   ○ across
9. ○ pagge   ○ pag   ○ page   ○ jage
10. ○ curcus   ○ circus   ○ sircus   ○ circuse

Do these problems. Be sure to look at the signs. If you have a calculator, use it to check your answers.

25 − 5 = _____	28 ÷ 4 = _____	11 x 11 = _____
6 x 1 = _____	14 ÷ 7 = _____	36 − 16 = _____
36 ÷ 6 = _____	16 + 6 = _____	18 ÷ 3 = _____
5 x 6 = _____	18 − 8 = _____	9 x 2 = _____
17 + 3 = _____	10 x 3 = _____	7 x 7 = _____
11 + 8 = _____	7 − 3 = _____	81 ÷ 9 = _____
19 − 4 = _____	22 − 2 = _____	24 + 12 = _____
4 x 2 = _____	7 x 6 = _____	54 ÷ 9 = _____
9 ÷ 3 = _____	3 x 7 = _____	93 − 10 = _____
12 ÷ 3 = _____	84 − 80 = _____	6 x 8 = _____

Probability and Statistics.

A scientist collected the following data on the length of the whales and dolphins that were studied:

blue whale	88 feet
humpback whale	54 feet
gray whale	39 feet
sperm whale	35 feet
beluga whale	13 feet
bottle-nosed dolphin.	9 feet
rough-toothed dolphin	8 feet
Atlantic spotted dolphin . . .	7 feet
spinner dolphin	7 feet

- The **range** is the difference between the highest number and the lowest number in the data.
- To calculate the **mean** (or average) add the list of numbers, and then divide by the number of items.
- The **median** is the middle number that appears in the data.
- The **mode** is the number that appears most often in the data.

1. What is the range of the data? _____

2. What is the median of the data? _____

3. What is the mode of the data? _____

Pancakes

In France, pancakes are called <u>crepes</u>. They are made with flour, eggs, and other things. They are usually rolled up with different kinds of food inside them. Most often, they are filled with fruit, such as blueberries, strawberries, and apples. In Mexico, pancakes are called <u>tortillas</u>. They are made with flour or cornmeal. The cornmeal is mixed up, and then the batter is poured onto a very hot griddle or pan. Tortillas are filled with a mixture of foods. Tortillas can also be folded to make <u>tacos</u>.

Write a recipe for your favorite pancakes and describe what you like to have on them.

_____

_____

_____

_____

_____

Use the probabilities below to describe whether the event is:

certain	likely	more likely	less likely	impossible

Penny has 11 pencils in her pencil box. Two pencils are orange,
3 pencils are blue, 5 pencils are yellow, and 1 pencil is green.

1. Pulling a **green** pencil from the box is _____ than pulling a **blue** pencil from the box.

2. Pulling a **yellow** pencil from the box is _____ than pulling a **green** pencil from the box.

3. Pulling a **black** pencil from the box is _____.

4. Pulling an **orange** pencil from the box is _____ than pulling a **blue** pencil from the box.

5. Penny has a new box of 12 pencils, and 12 of the pencils are yellow. Pulling a **yellow** pencil from the new box is _____.

Subtract to find the differences.

5,042 −1,624	2,710 −1,624	4,200 −1,122	7,106 −2,410	3,340 −1,112	9,824 −1,224
6,831 −4,560	7,605 −1,282	6,351 −5,675	8,001 −2,381	4,232 − 624	1,898 − 197
2,356 −2,147	9,010 −2,167	3,542 −1,004	5,600 −2,983	7,575 − 58	4,230 −1,606

Commas in a series give meaning to a sentence. Put an X next to the correct sentence.

1. Five children went on a bus to the zoo.

_____Jeannie, Julie Ann, John, Dennis, and Dave went together.

_____Jeannie, Julie, Ann, John, Dennis, and Dave went together.

2. There are three things to eat for lunch today.

_____We have chicken, sandwiches, carrot sticks, and soup.

_____We have chicken sandwiches, carrot sticks, and soup.

3. "I want to know where John is," Henry said.

_____"Where is John Henry?"

_____"Where is John, Henry?"

4. Ted can't find his four sisters.

_____Mary Ellen, Sue Tanya, Rachel, and Lisa are hiding.

_____Mary, Ellen, Sue, Tanya, Rachel, and Lisa are hiding.

Read the main idea sentence and the details below. Put an X before each detail important to the main idea.

One Saturday, Mike took his little sister, Judy, for a walk.

_____ They walked around the paths of the big housing project.

_____ There, on a weed, was a big, fat, green caterpillar.

_____ They knew they mustn't walk on the fresh, green grass of the lawns.

_____ They could hunt under the hedges along the walks for beetles, ants, and earthworms.

_____ They showed their friend, Jake, the caterpillar.

Look at these words and use them to fill in the blanks.

enough	tube	fantastic	where
woman	through	daughter	

1. Which word ends with the same sound as <u>lipstick</u>? _____

2. Which word begins the same as <u>what</u>? _____

3. Which word has the same vowel sound as <u>too</u>? _____

4. Write the spelling words that make pairs with the following words:

son _____   man _____

5. Write the spelling word that ends with the same sound as <u>off</u>. _____

6. What word ends with the same sound as <u>chew</u>? _____

Floating Eggs

The water in the Great Salt Lake allows you to float much more easily than regular water or even salty ocean water. How is that possible?

Stuff You Need:

2 2-cup drinking glasses or measuring cups
2 hard-boiled eggs
salt
measuring spoons
water

Here's What to Do:

1. Pour 5 ounces of warm water into each cup.

2. Gently lower one egg into a cup. Observe what happens.

3. Add about 5 tablespoons of salt to the other cup and stir. Gently lower the other egg into this solution. Does it float? If it doesn't, then keep adding salt, a tablespoon at a time, stirring very gently, until the egg finally floats. How much salt did it take?

4. Take the egg out of the salt solution. Keep adding salt, a tablespoon at a time, until the salt doesn't dissolve in the water anymore. How much salt did you put in before this happened?

What's This All About?

When the salt dissolves in the water, its molecules split into two tiny particles. These particles are small enough to slightly nudge the water molecules aside and slide into the spaces between the larger water molecules. Since this packs more matter into the same space, the saltwater becomes more dense than freshwater.

As you add salt to the water, the water will become so dense that it will not hold any more salt. Think of it as having filled all of the spaces between the molecules so that there is nowhere else for the salt to go. If more salt is added, it just sinks to the bottom undissolved. The solution is said to be saturated.

Different liquids have different **densities**. The amount of matter packed into an area determines the density of a material. And the same amounts of two liquids can have different weights. Liquids that are not very dense will float on liquids that are more dense. Oil, for example, weighs less than the same amount of water. This is why oil floats on water. Also, the liquids that are more dense exert a greater buoyant force (ability to make an object float) on objects than do liquids that are less dense.

Stacking Books

Why would books stacked on top of each other and hanging over the edge of a table stay there? Why wouldn't they fall? Stack away and find out.

Stuff You Need:

5 books
table

Here's What to Do:

1. Place a book on the edge of the table. Place the second book on top of the first book, letting it hang one inch over the edge of the table.

2. Continue this process, adding the other three books until the top book is way out over the edge.

What's This All About?

As the books are stacked on top of each other, they start to function as a single object. Think of yourself running alone. All of a sudden, a bunch of friends join you, and then you are running along holding hands. Once you start holding hands, you are a unit working together.

As the books stack on top of each other, they become a unit, too. The center of gravity is at the center of that unit (the stack), and that center point is resting on the table–not over the edge. That is why the top one can stick way out over the edge and not fall off the table.

Activity Sheet:

Draw a picture of your stack of books on the table; then draw a vertical line through the center of the stack to indicate the center of gravity.

Section 1

Page 3

Page 4

Page 5

Page 6

Page 7

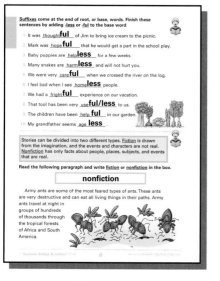

Page 8

Page 9

Page 10

Page 11

Day 5

Place Value. Write the numbers.

6 tens 8 ones	9 ones 4 tens	5 tens 0 ones	10 tens 0 ones
68	**49**	**50**	**10**
6 tens 3 hundreds 8 ones	4 hundreds 0 tens 2 ones	5 ones 6 hundreds 7 tens	9 hundreds 3 ones 5 tens
368	**402**	**675**	**953**

Write these numbers.

8. five hundred sixty-one **561**
9. four hundred eighty-six **486**
10. two hundred ninety-nine **299**
11. eight hundred **800**
12. one hundred fifty **150**

How many gumballs in each set?

Ex. **221**
13. **411**
14. **213**
15. **330**

Divide these compound words into three categories. Write in cursive.

skyline, grapevine, raindrop, hindsight, drumstick, bluebell, landscape, oatmeal, suitcase, wishbone, hitchhike, themselves, limestone, thumbtack

1. long vowel combinations
skyline, grapevine, hindsight, oatmeal, suitcase, limestone

2. short vowel combinations
drumstick, themselves, thumbtack

3. long and short vowel combinations
raindrop, bluebell, landscape, wishbone, hitchhike

Page 12

Write a word for each clue.

knead   sense   praise   dull   guide
wheat   purchase   numb   certain   amazing

1. not able to feel — **numb**
2. we do this to dough — **knead**
3. to be sure — **certain**
4. to buy something — **purchase**
5. to see, hear, feel, taste, smell — **sense**
6. flour is made from — **wheat**
7. a leader of a group — **guide**
8. to say something nice — **praise**
9. something wonderful can be — **amazing**
10. a knife that is not sharp — **dull**

FACTOID Coughing can make air move through your windpipe at over a thousand feet per second!

Haiku is a form of Japanese poetry that follows a special pattern of 17 syllables. There are 5 syllables in the first line, 7 in the second line, and 5 in the third line. Most haiku poetry is about nature.

Read the following haiku poem.

Flakes of snow outside.
Icicles hanging from eaves.
Winter is now here.

Use the lines to write a haiku poem of your own about apples, summer, or anything you want.

Answers will vary.

Page 13

Day 6

How many ways can you make the amount of money shown in these problems? Use real money to help you.

Ex. 10¢
10 pennies
2 nickels
1 nickel, 5 pennies
1 dime

1. 25¢
2. $1.00
3. $1.60

Answers will vary.

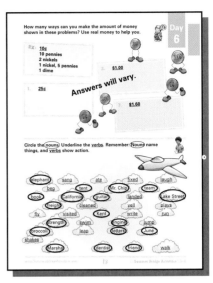

Circle the nouns. Underline the verbs. Remember: Nouns name things, and verbs show action.

elephant, sang, ate, fixed, laugh, beg, tent, Mr. Chip, team, book, California, guitar, landed, Lake Street, freight, cleaned, Kent, yell, write, plays, fly, visited, swim, engine, jump, June, strength, leap, letters, broccoli, shakes, Marsha, dentist, friend, walk

Page 14

Use the Word Bank to make compound words matching the descriptions.

Word Bank

bath	apple
team	tub
horse	storm
snow	back
scare	side
post	card
hill	mates
pine	crow

Ex. A place your mom sends you to get clean. **bathtub**
1. A fruit that is good to eat. **pineapple**
2. What farmers put in cornfields to scare birds away. **scarecrow**
3. A kind of weather some people get in the wintertime. **snowstorm**
4. If you ride on a horse, you have this kind of ride. **horseback**
5. A place that might be grassy, high up, and a good place for a picnic. **hillside**
6. A type of mail you can write and send to a friend. **postcard**
7. People who play sports with you. **teammates**

You are lost in the forest for a long time with nothing but a knife, a few matches, and one pan. How and where will you live? What will you do? What will you eat?

Answers will vary.

Page 15

Day 7

Rounding Numbers. Round to the nearest ten.

EXAMPLE: 28 = 20 or 30
30, because 28 is nearer to 30 than to 20.

65 = 60 or 70
70, because when a number is halfway, round it up to the larger number.

12 = 10 or 20
10, because 12 is nearer to 10 than it is to 20.

Circle the answer.

1. 63 = 60 or 70
2. 19 = 10 or 20
3. 55 = 50 or 60
4. 83 = 80 or 90

5. 27 = 20 or 30
6. 99 = 90 or 100
7. 25 = 20 or 30
8. 12 = 10 or 20

Write the answer.

9. 28 = **30**
10. 43 = **40**
11. 14 = **10**
12. 85 = **90**

13. 33 = **30**
14. 90 = **90**
15. 78 = **80**
16. 20 = **20**

Round to the nearest 100.

Ex. 297 = **300**
16. 211 = 200 or 300
17. 767 = 700 or 800
18. 841 = **800**
19. 587 = **600**

Rewrite this paragraph. Add the correct punctuation and capitalization.

last summer we went camping in colorado we went hiking and swimming every day one time i actually saw a little deer with spots and a white tail we also collected a lot of pretty rocks flowers and leaves we had a great time i didnt want to leave

Last summer, we went camping in Colorado. We went hiking and swimming every day. One time, I actually saw a little deer with spots and a white tail. We also collected a lot of pretty rocks, flowers, and leaves. We had a great time. I didnt want to leave.

Page 16

Circle the word that is divided into syllables correctly.

FACTOID The state of Florida is larger than the country of England.

EXAMPLE: fif/teen   fit/teen   fift/een   fifte/en

1. cact/us   ca/ctus   cac/tus   c/actus
2. bli/ster   blist/er   blis/ter   bl/ister
3. al/ways   a/lways   alw/ays   alwa/ys
4. har/bor   ha/rbor   harb/or   harbo/r
5. fl/ower   flo/wer   flowe/r   flow/er
6. bas/ket   ba/sket   bask/et   baske/t
7. e/nclose   en/close   encl/ose   enclo/se
8. obe/ys   o/beys   ob/eys   obey/s

Write the abbreviations for the following words. Be sure to put a period (.) at the end of each abbreviation. Write in cursive.

EXAMPLE:
1. January — *Jan.*
3. February — **Feb.**
5. March — **Mar.**
7. April — **Apr.**
9. August — **Aug.**
11. October — **Oct.**
13. November — **Nov.**
15. December — **Dec.**

2. Sunday — **Sun.**
4. Monday — **Mon.**
6. Tuesday — **Tues.**
8. Wednesday — **Wed.**
10. Thursday — **Thur.**
12. Saturday — **Sat.**
14. Doctor — **Dr.**
16. Mister — **Mr.**

Page 17

Day 8

Be sure to look at the ones, tens, hundreds, and thousands as you do the following problems.

Which number is greater? Circle your answer.

1. 126 / 261
2. 342 / 231
3. 619 / 718
4. 426 / 1,326
5. 2,510 / 3,511
6. 1,629 / 1,639

Circle the number that is less.

7. 580 / 579
8. 999 / 899
9. 624 / 524
10. 1,200 / 1,327
11. 7,824 / 7,842
12. 5,559 / 5,846

Write greater than (>) or less than (<) on the line.

Ex. 521 is **>** than 121
13. 267 is **>** than 367
14. 126 is **<** than 226
15. 808 is **>** than 801
16. 429 is **>** than 249
17. 762 is **>** than 761
18. 1,638 is **>** than 738
19. 4,206 is **<** than 5,206
20. 3,929 is **>** than 3,729

Read the following words. Write the vowel you hear and mark if it's long or short.

EXAMPLE: fly — i long   went — e short

1. tie — **i long**
2. trail — **a long**
3. sweat — **e short**
4. puzzle — **u short**
5. chief — **e long**
6. bump — **u short**
7. head — **e short**
8. mule — **u long**
9. knot — **o short**
10. niece — **e long**
11. toad — **o long**
12. ripped — **i short**
13. bugle — **u long**
14. neck — **e short**
15. find — **i long**
16. plan — **a short**
17. high — **i long**
18. chip — **i short**

Page 18

Use commas, add small words, or leave words out to combine the sentences.

FACTOID A piece of square, dry paper can't be folded in half more than seven times.

1. My friends' names are Wanda and Pete. I also like Mandy and Joe.
I like my friends, Wanda, Pete, Mandy, and Joe.
2. Rats will chew on wood and bones. They also will chew on nuts and twigs.
Rats chew on wood, bones, nuts, and twigs.
3. Dogs and cats can be pets. Gerbils and hamsters can be pets, too.
Dogs, cats, gerbils, and hamsters can be pets.
4. I am wearing blue jeans and a striped shirt. My shoes are black, and my socks are green. On my head is a baseball cap.
I am wearing blue jeans, a striped shirt, black shoes, green socks, and a baseball cap.

Read the directions through completely first. If you follow the directions carefully, you will find the name of an animal.

P L A E N H T E

1. Remove the letter L and the last E.
2. Put the LE at the beginning of the word.
3. Move the second E so it is at the beginning of the word.
4. Put an S at the end of the word.
5. Move the H so that it is between the P and the A.
6. Don't skip step 4.
7. Write the name of the animal here.
ELEPHANT

Page 19

Day 9

Match the names with the shapes.

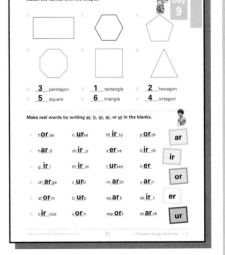

A. **3** pentagon
B. **1** rectangle
C. **2** hexagon
D. **5** square
E. **6** triangle
F. **4** octagon

Make real words by writing ar, ir, or, or ur in the blanks.

1. h**or**se   n**ur**se   th**ir**ty   p**or**ch
2. h**ar**d   ch**ir**p   s**er**ve   b**ir**ch
3. g**ir**l   th**ir**st   t**ur**key   h**er**
4. ch**ar**ge   c**ur**b   m**ar**ch   y**ar**n
5. st**or**m   b**ur**p   sp**ar**k   sk**ir**t
6. c**ir**cus   c**or**n   rep**or**t   st**ar**ch

ar   ir   or   er   ur

Page 20

Build a super sandwich with the clues given and the ingredients listed.

Ingredients

pickles	ham	bologna	wheat bread
lettuce	beef	butter	sourdough bread
tomatoes	chicken	mustard	white bread
bean sprouts	pork	mayonnaise	rye bread

Clues

1. Make the sandwich using one kind of bread, two vegetables, and two meats.
2. Two ingredients should start with b and two with p.
3. Use the spread with the most letters in it.
4. Don't use anything that starts with wh or anything that ends in f.
5. Add a mystery ingredient. List the ingredients of your sandwich:
   Answers will vary.

Draw and color your sandwich.

Answers will vary.

Put commas where they belong in the sentences.

EXAMPLE: August 10, 1970, and May 10, 1973, are birth dates in our family.

1. My parents were married in Portland, Oregon, on May 1, 1959.
2. We had chicken, potatoes, corn, gravy, and ice cream for dinner.
3. George Washington became the first president on April 30, 1789.
4. Sam was born June 16, 1947, in Rome, Italy.
5. We saw deer, bear, elk, and goats on our trip.
6. On July 24, 1962, in Boise, Idaho, I won the big race.

Write your own series of words in these sentences. Put in the commas.

7. My favorite desserts are *Answers will vary.*
8. Some of my relatives are

Page 21

Day 10

Column Addition.

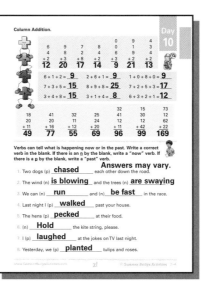

6	9	7	8	0	9	4
3	9	8	4	6	1	3
+2	+2	+2	+2	+3	+2	+2
12	20	17	14	9	21	13

6+1+2 = **9**   2+6+1 = **9**   1+0+8+0 = **9**

7+3+5 = **15**   8+9+8 = **25**   7+2+5+3 = **17**

3+4+8 = **15**   3+1+4 = **8**   6+3+2+2 = **13**

18	41	32	25	41	30	12
20	20	11	24	12	12	62
+11	+16	+12	+20	+43	+42	+22
49	77	55	69	96	99	169

Verbs can tell what is happening now or in the past. Write a correct verb in the blank. If there is an n by the blank, write a "now" verb. If there is a p by the blank, write a "past" verb.

Answers may vary.

1. Two dogs (p) **chased** each other down the road.
2. The wind is (n) **is blowing** and the trees (n) **are swaying**.
3. We can (n) **run** and (n) **be fast** in the race.
4. Last night I (p) **walked** past your house.
5. The hens (p) **pecked** at their food.
6. (n) **Hold** the kite string, please.
7. I (p) **laughed** at the jokes on TV last night.
8. Yesterday, we (p) **planted** tulips and roses.

Page 22

FACTOID
The average yawn lasts about six seconds.

Fill in the blanks with words that begin with bl-, fl-, br-, cl-, sn-, gl-, st-, cr-, sk-, gr-, or sp-.

Answers may vary.

1. A big **black skunk** was in the middle of the road.
2. Sid swept the floor with a **broom** after he spilled the **bread** crumbs on it.
3. The **flag** pole was in the middle of a **flower** bed.
4. The time on the **clock** gave us a **clue** to the answer.
5. A **snake** slithered along the cold **ground**.
6. Rick fixed the broken **glass** with some **glue**.
7. The robber **stole** a **bracelet** from the **store**.
8. The baby colored on her **crib** with a blue **crayon**.
9. Jane ripped her **skirt** as she **stood** by the fence.
10. The **crops** were very **green** this summer.

bl-
fl-
br-

sp-	gr-	sk-	cr-	st-	gl-	sn-	cl-

Do some research on toads, frogs, and tadpoles. Use the Internet or an encyclopedia. Then, draw six pictures to show, in order, how tadpoles change into frogs or toads.

1. _____ 2. _____

3. _____   *Answers will vary.*

5. _____ 6. _____

Page 23

Day 11

Write the numbers that come after, before, or between.

1. 58, **59**, 60
2. 80, **81**, 82
3. _**18**_, 19, 20
4. _**16**_, 17, 18
5. _**9**_, 10, **11**
6. 151, **152**, 153
7. 429, **430**, **431**
8. 869, **870**, 871

9. 619, **620**, **621**
10. 887, **888**, **889**
11. 499, **500**, **501**
12. 209, **210**, **211**
13. 721, **722**, 723
14. 305, **306**, 307
15. 199, **200**, 201
16. 998, 999, **1,000**

17. **1,200**, 1,201
18. 2,429, **2,430**
19. 6,000, **6,001**
20. 9,929, **9,930**
21. 3,999, 4,000
22. 7,822, **7,823**
23. 7,841, 7,842
24. 9,999, **10,000**

Complete each sentence using more than, less than, or equal to. Write your answer on the line.

Rules:

2 cups = 1 pint
2 pints = 1 quart
4 quarts = 1 gallon

EXAMPLE:
Is one cup greater than, less than, or equal to 1 pint?
If 2 cups = 1 pint,
then 1 cup is **less than** 1 pint.

A. 2 pints are **equal to** 1 quart.
B. 1 pint is **less than** 1 quart.
C. 3 quarts are **less than** 1 gallon.
D. 3 cups are **less than** 1 quart.
E. 1 gallon is **more than** 1 pint.
F. 6 pints are **equal to** 3 quarts.
G. 2 pints are **equal to** 4 cups.
H. 8 quarts are **equal to** 2 gallons.

Page 24

FACTOID
The welwitschia plant from Africa looks a bit like an octopus and lives for about 1,000 years.

Read the paragraph and circle the answers to the questions.

Many enormous bones have been found. Scientists have put them together to make dinosaur skeletons. Fossils of other extinct animals and plants have also been found. You can see dinosaur skeletons and other fossils in many museums.

1. The main idea of the paragraph is
   a. museums.
   b. **fossils.**
   c. animals.

2. The word them in the paragraph stands for
   a. skeletons.
   b. dinosaurs.
   c. **bones.**

3. The word enormous means
   a. **huge.**
   b. hungry.
   c. little.

4. In this paragraph, extinct means
   a. happy to be alive.
   b. **not alive anymore.**
   c. very big animals.

Study these words and fill in the blanks with the correct words.

night
different
dry
knock
famous
snow
hopped
walk
pear
oxygen

1. Which word begins with a silent letter? **knock**
2. This is a weather word. **snow**
3. Which word has a t sound at the end, but it is not the letter t making the sound? **hopped**
4. Which word has a silent gh? **night**
5. Which word means "well-known"? **famous**
6. Which word has the short o sound, but the letter is not an o? **walk**
7. What do we breathe? **oxygen**
8. Which word has three syllables? **different**
9. Which word sounds the same as pair? **pear**
10. A word that ends with a long i sound. **dry**

Page 25

Day 12

See if you can figure out these story problems.

1. How many days are between the 18th and the 28th day of the month? **9 days**

2. If Ted is next to last in line, and he is also tenth from the first person in line, how many children are in line? **11 children**

3. Twenty-five children are in line. Only one is a girl. She is in the middle of the line. How many boys are in front of her, and how many are in back of her? **12 boys**

There are 20 horses in a race. Prince is next to last. Name his place in the race. **19th**

If today was the 22nd of June, what date will it be one week from today? **29th**

Jack is 16th in line. How many people are ahead of him? **15 people**

The subject of a sentence tells who or what the sentence is about. The predicate of a sentence tells something about the subject. Both can have more than one word or just one word.

Circle the subject of each sentence and underline the predicate.

EXAMPLE: (Our team) won the game.

1. (Clowns) make me laugh.
2. (We) started to swim.
3. (Chris) worked in his garden.
4. (Bees) can sting people.
5. (Mom and I) rode our horses.
6. (Chickens) lay eggs daily.
7. (Ducks) eat lots of worms.

8. (A little red fox) ran by us.
9. (April) lost her house keys.
10. (Lions) live in cages.
11. (I) found twenty-five cents.
12. (This ruler) is one foot long.
13. (We) went on a picnic.
14. (Birds) make nests for their eggs.
15. (The king) rode a bike.

Page 26

FACTOID
Scientists are trying to grow vaccines in fruit so you can eat the cure instead of getting a shot!

Write the word that does not belong with the other words in the row. Then describe why the other words belong together.

EXAMPLE:

rose, daisy, lazy, tulip, lily	*lazy*	*others are flowers*

1. newspaper, book, television, magazine — **television** others you can read
2. hand, eye, foot, hose — **hose** others are parts of the body
3. tuba, clarinet, jazz, flute, harp — **jazz** others are instruments
4. tire, hammer, screwdriver, wrench — **tire** others are tools
5. robin, hawk, sparrow, pig, jay — **pig** others are birds
6. John, Tom, Robert, Jenny, Todd — **Jenny** others are male
7. Moon, Mars, Earth, Pluto, Venus — **Moon** others are planets
8. lettuce, peach, carrot, peas, beets — **peach** others are vegetables
9. Mary, Jane, Susan, Ann, George — **George** others are female

Use the apostrophe correctly. Change each underlined word or phrase by using the apostrophe.

EXAMPLE:

1. You are a good piano player. — *You're*
2. This is my grandmothers pet dog. — grandmother's
3. The monsters eyes are green. — monster's
4. The boy will not make his bed. — won't
5. The girl would not help her friend. — wouldn't
6. I borrowed Nancys swimming suit. — Nancy's
7. Boyd does not have a catchers mitt. — catcher's
8. It is so hot during the summer. — It's

Page 27

Day 13

Adding 2-Digit Numbers. Remember to trade or regroup.

EXAMPLE:
```
  1
 26
+37
 63
```

62	18	45	73	42	19
+19	+27	+38	+19	+29	+9
81	45	83	92	71	28

56	66	14	37	16	38	29
+57	+55	+26	+33	+85	+32	+55
113	121	40	70	101	70	84

96¢	46¢	98¢	95¢	56¢	17¢	11¢
+56¢	+64¢	+84¢	+85¢	+26¢	+17¢	+99¢
$1.52	$1.10	$1.82	$1.80	82¢	34¢	$1.10

Read the sentences carefully. Look at the underlined word in each sentence. Choose another word or words that mean the same as the underlined word.

EXAMPLE:
Will you repay the money I lent you? — *return*

1. The oak tree is afire.
2. Sara fell down outside, but she was unhurt.
3. I would like to revisit Disneyland sometime.
4. Do not uncover the dough, or it will dry out.
5. Don't use this phone; it's only for incoming calls.
6. This paper is really important.
7. This part of the forest remains untouched.
8. Every few years we repaint the school.
9. I dislike cake and ice cream.

Answers will vary.

Page 28

Add suffixes to the following words. Use -est, -tion, or -ty. At the end, write three sentences. Choose three different words with three different suffixes. Remember to double, drop, or change some letters.

1. taste — *tastiest*
2. safe — **safety/safest**
3. prepare — **preparation**
4. sad — **saddest**
5. dirt — **dirtiest/dirty**
6. act — **action**
7. hungry — **hungriest**
8. heavy — **heaviest**
9. direct — **direction**
10. invent — **invention**

1. _____
2. _____

Answers will vary.

Is and are tell that something is happening now. Use is with singular subjects and are with plural subjects.

1. Max and I **are** best friends.
2. Bill **is** also our friend.
3. We **are** all going camping this summer.
4. Meg **is** coming with us.
5. Her sister **is** coming, too.
6. Those bananas **are** very ripe.

is / are

Write your own sentences now. Write two using is and two using are.

1. is _____
2. are _____   *Sentences will vary.*
3. is _____
4. are _____

Page 29

Day 14

Arrange the numbers from greatest to least.
1. 261 325 496 547 → **547 496 325 261**
2. 746 793 733 779 → **793 779 746 733**
3. 596 579 588 499 → **596 588 579 499**
4. 496 649 964 946 → **964 946 649 496**
5. 846 808 903 778 → **903 846 808 778**

Arrange the numbers from least to greatest.
1. 764 674 746 647 → **647 674 746 764**
2. 503 530 353 550 → **353 503 530 550**
3. 940 490 904 409 → **409 490 904 940**
4. 883 838 388 880 → **388 838 880 883**
5. 676 767 690 719 → **676 690 719 767**

Write these words in alphabetical order. Be sure to look at the first, second, and third letters. Write them in cursive.

wash, large, enough, school, brought, front, eye, spread, people, do, often, breakfast, does, you, neighbor

1. breakfast
2. brought
3. do
4. does
5. enough
6. eye
7. front
8. large
9. neighbor
10. often
11. people
12. school
13. spread
14. wash
15. you

Page 30

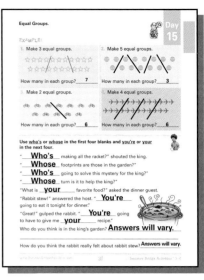

FACTOID A regulation baseball has 108 stitches.

Sequence.

Denise and Grayson washed their dad's car. First, they filled a bucket with soapy water. Denise got some old rags from the house while Grayson got the hose. They put soapy water all over the car and washed off the dirt. Next, they sprayed the car with water. To finish the job, Denise and Grayson wiped the car dry with some clean towels. Both of them were surprised when their dad gave them each $5.

Write four sentences about the story in the correct order.
1.
2.
3.
4.
Answers will vary.

The words below contain suffixes such as -est, -tion, and -ty. Read each one and write the base word on the line.

EXAMPLE:
1. safety — *safe*
2. hungriest — **hungry**
4. invention — **invent**
7. location — **locate**
10. loveliest — **lovely**
11. preparation — **prepare**
13. reality — **real**
15. hottest — **hot**
3. starvation — **starve**
6. action — **act**
9. certainty — **certain**
12. direction — **direct**
10. saddest — **sad**
12. tasty — **taste**
14. suggestion — **suggest**
16. wettest — **wet**

Page 31

Day 15

Equal Groups.

EXAMPLE:
1. Make 3 equal groups. How many in each group? **7**
2. Make 5 equal groups. How many in each group? **3**
3. Make 2 equal groups. How many in each group? **6**
4. Make 4 equal groups. How many in each group? **6**

Use who's or whose in the first four blanks and you're or your in the next four.

"**Who's** making all the racket?" shouted the king.
"**Whose** footprints are those in the garden?"
"**Who's** going to solve this mystery for the king?"
"**Whose** turn is it to help the king?"
"What is **your** favorite food?" asked the dinner guest.
"Rabbit stew!" answered the host. "**You're** going to eat it tonight for dinner."
"Great!" gulped the rabbit. "**You're** going to have to give me **your** recipe." **Answers will vary.**
Who do you think is in the king's garden? **Answers will vary.**
How do you think the rabbit really felt about rabbit stew? **Answers will vary.**

Page 32

Follow the directions. **Some answers will vary.**

FACTOID Glue was once made by boiling animal bones, hides, and hooves. Today, we use synthetic substances.

1. Get a dictionary.
2. Look at any page between 40 and 55. Page_____
3. Write down the guide words.
4. Words in a dictionary are in **alphabetical** order.
5. Write the meaning of the guide word on the right-hand side of the page you are looking at.
6. How many syllables does your guide word have? _____
7. In your dictionary, what mark shows where words are divided? **/**
8. Find a word on the page you are looking at that has three syllables. Write it down, and in your own words, define it.
9. The guide words show the **first** and the **last** entry words on the page.

Making "Clipped" Words from Longer Words. Try making these words into clipped words.

EXAMPLE: auto/mobile → **Clipped Word**

1. I can't believe that Grayson can eat four hamburgers! — *burgers*
2. When Andy grows up, he wants to fly airplanes. — **planes**
3. When Denise went to New York, she rode in a taxicab. — **taxi or cab**
4. A hippopotamus can hold its breath for a long time. — **hippo**
5. Have you ever been inside a submarine? — **sub**
6. Spectators filled the stadium at the baseball game. — **ball**
7. Lori loves talking with her grandmother on the telephone. — **phone**
8. Matt was amazed by the photograph in the art gallery. — **photo**

Section 2

Page 37

Day 1

Find the differences. Be sure to trade or regroup.

EXAMPLE:
80−29=51	71−7=65	64−57=**7**	23−9=**14**	70−23=**47**	43−14=**29**	77−28=**49**
63−45=**18**	91−42=**49**	38−19=**19**	81−15=**66**	55−9=**46**	82−16=**66**	25−16=**9**
68−39=**29**	76−37=**39**	75−68=**68**	85−17=**68**	50−24=**26**	31−15=**16**	44−36=**8**

Go to the library and get a book you have not read. After you finish reading it, write a book report. Use the outline below to help you.

1. Title
2. Author
3. Main characters
4. Setting: Where does the story take place?
5. Main idea: What is the book about?
Answers will vary.
6. Did you like the book? _____ Why or why not?

Page 38

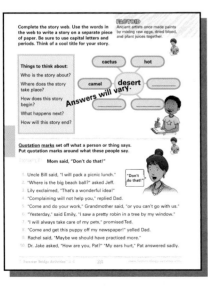

Complete the story web. Use the words in the web to write a story on a separate piece of paper. Be sure to use capital letters and periods. Think of a cool title for your story.

FACTOID Ancient artists once made paints by mixing raw eggs, dried blood, and plant juices together.

Things to think about:
Who is the story about?
Where does the story take place?
How does this story begin?
What happens next?
How will this story end?

cactus, hot, camel, desert — **Answers will vary.**

Quotation marks set off what a person or thing says. Put quotation marks around what these people say.

EXAMPLE: Mom said, "Don't do that!"

1. Uncle Bill said, "I will pack a picnic lunch."
2. "Where is the big beach ball?" asked Jeff.
3. Lily exclaimed, "That's a wonderful idea!"
4. "Complaining will not help you," replied Dad.
5. "Come and do your work," Grandmother said, "or you can't go with us."
6. "Yesterday," said Emily, "I saw a pretty robin in a tree by my window."
7. "I will always take care of my pets," promised Ted.
8. "Come and get this puppy off my newspaper!" yelled Dad.
9. Rachel said, "Maybe we should have practiced more."
10. Dr. Jake asked, "How are you, Pat?" "My ears hurt," Pat answered sadly.

Page 39

Day 2

Using Grids.

Which fruit is located at 3, 4? **apple**
Put a circle around the fruit located at 2, 2.
Draw a peach on 5, 3.
Which fruit is located at 5, 5? **strawberry**
Where is the pear located? **1,1**
Put a box around the fruit located at 4, 2.

Which shape is located at 5, 5? **diamond**
Where is the square located? **2,2**
Draw a circle around the shape located at 3, 4.
Draw a line to connect the shapes located at 4, 1 and 1, 5.

Common nouns are general names for places, things, and people. Proper nouns name a specific person, place, or thing and begin with a capital letter.

Put these nouns under the right heading and then write two of your own. Be sure to use capital letters on the proper nouns.

salt lake, monday, pet, day, november, mr. brown, boston, beans, apple, school, dog, ocean, oak street, class, holiday, christmas, boat, rex, florida, dr. phil

Proper Nouns	Common Nouns
Mrs. Jones	teacher
Salt Lake	pet
Monday	day
November	beans
Mr. Brown	apple
Boston	school
Oak Street	dog
Christmas	ocean
Rex	class
Florida	holiday
Dr. Phil	boat
Answers will vary.	

Page 40

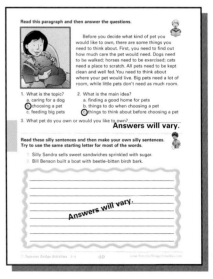

Read this paragraph and then answer the questions.

Before you decide what kind of pet you would like to own, there are some things you need to think about. First, you need to find out how much care the pet would need. Dogs need to be walked; horses need to be exercised; cats need a place to scratch. All pets need to be kept clean and well fed. You need to think about where your pet would live. Big pets need a lot of room, while little pets don't need as much room.

1. What is the topic?
   a. caring for a dog
   b. choosing a pet *(circled)*
   c. feeding big pets

2. What is the main idea?
   a. finding a good home for pets
   b. things to do when choosing a pet
   c. things to think about before choosing a pet *(circled)*

3. What pet do you own or would you like to own? **Answers will vary.**

Read these silly sentences and then make your own silly sentences. Try to use the same starting letter for most of the words.
1. Silly Sandra sells sweet sandwiches sprinkled with sugar.
2. Bill Benson built a boat with beetle-bitten birch bark.

Answers will vary.

Page 41

Add or subtract. Check the signs. Trade or regroup if you need to.

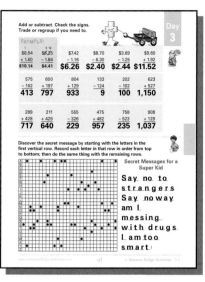

EXAMPLE!

$8.54	$6.25	$7.42	$8.70	$3.69	$9.60
+ 1.60	− 1.84	− 1.16	− 6.30	− 1.25	+ 1.92
$10.14	$4.41	$6.26	$2.40	$2.44	$11.52

575	600	804	133	202	623
− 162	+ 197	+ 129	− 124	− 102	+ 527
413	797	933	9	100	1,150

289	211	555	475	758	908
+ 428	+ 429	− 326	+ 482	− 523	+ 129
717	640	229	957	235	1,037

Discover the secret message by starting with the letters in the first vertical row. Record each letter in that row in order from top to bottom; then do the same thing with the remaining rows.

Secret Messages for a Super Kid

Say no to strangers Say no way am I messing with drugs. I am too smart!

Page 42

Sequencing. Read this story; then number the sentences in the order they happened.

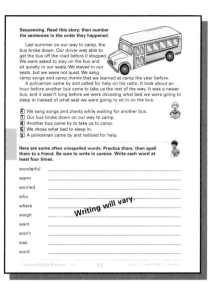

Last summer on our way to camp, the bus broke down. Our driver was able to get the bus off the road before it stopped. We were asked to stay on the bus and sit quietly in our seats. We stayed in our seats, but we were not quiet. We sang camp songs and camp chants that we learned at camp the year before.

A policeman came by and called for help on his radio. It took about an hour before another bus came to take us the rest of the way. It was a newer bus, and it wasn't long before we were choosing what bed we were going to sleep in instead of what seat we were going to sit in on the bus.

2 We sang songs and chants while waiting for another bus.
1 Our bus broke down on our way to camp.
4 Another bus came by to take us to camp.
5 We chose what bed to sleep in.
3 A policeman came by and radioed for help.

Here are some often misspelled words. Practice them; then spell them to a friend. Be sure to write in cursive. Write each word at least four times.

wonderful
warm
worried
who
where
weigh
want
won't
was
word

Writing will vary.

Page 43

Ways of Writing the Same Concept. Circle the correct answers to the problems. There will be more than one answer for each one.

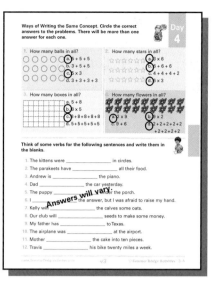

1. How many balls in all?
   a. 5 + 5 + 5
   b. 3 + 5 + 5
   c. 5 × 3
   d. 3 + 3 + 3 + 3

2. How many stars in all?
   a. 3 × 6
   b. 6 + 6 + 6
   c. 4 + 4 + 4 + 2
   d. 9 × 3

3. How many boxes in all?
   a. 5 + 8
   b. 8 × 5
   c. 8 + 8 + 8 + 8 + 8
   d. 5 + 5 + 5 + 5

4. How many flowers in all?
   a. 2 × 9
   b. 9 × 2
   c. 2 + 2 + 2 + 2 + 2 + 2 + 2 + 2 + 2

Think of some verbs for the following sentences and write them in the blanks.

1. The kittens were _____ in circles.
2. The parakeets have _____ all their food.
3. Andrew is _____ the piano.
4. Dad _____ the car yesterday.
5. The puppy _____ the porch.
6. I _____ the answer, but I was afraid to raise my hand.
7. Kelly will _____ the calves some oats.
8. Our club will _____ seeds to make some money.
9. My father has _____ to Texas.
10. The airplane was _____ at the airport.
11. Mother _____ the cake into ten pieces.
12. Travis _____ his bike twenty miles a week.

Answers will vary.

Page 44

Choose the correct homophone to complete the sentence.

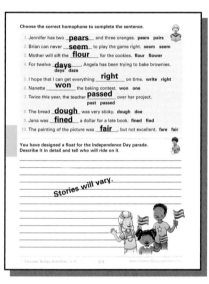

1. Jennifer has two **pears** and three oranges. pears pairs
2. Brian can never **seem** to play the game right. seem seam
3. Mother will sift the **flour** for the cookies. flour flower
4. For twelve **days** Angela has been trying to bake brownies. days daze
5. I hope that I can get everything **right** on time. write right
6. Nanette **won** the baking contest. won one
7. Twice this year, the teacher **passed** over her project. past passed
8. The bread **dough** was very sticky. dough doe
9. Jana was **fined** a dollar for a late book. fined find
10. The painting of the picture was **fair**, but not excellent. fare fair

You have designed a float for the Independence Day parade. Describe it in detail and tell who will ride on it.

Stories will vary.

Page 45

Thinking about Time.

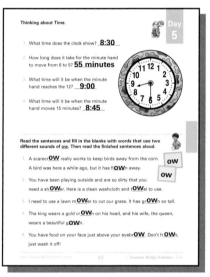

1. What time does the clock show? **8:30**
2. How long does it take for the minute hand to move from 6 to 5? **55 minutes**
3. What time will it be when the minute hand reaches the 12? **9:00**
4. What time will it be when the minute hand moves 15 minutes? **8:45**

Read the sentences and fill in the blanks with words that use two different sounds of ow. Then read the finished sentences aloud.

1. A scarecr**ow** really works to keep birds away from the corn. A bird was here a while ago, but it has fl**ow**n away.
2. You have been playing outside and are so dirty that you need a sh**ow**er. Here is a clean washcloth and t**ow**el to use.
3. I need to use a lawn m**ow**er to cut our grass. It has gr**ow**n so tall.
4. The king wears a gold cr**ow**n on his head, and his wife, the queen, wears a beautiful g**ow**n.
5. You have food on your face just above your eyebr**ow**. Don't fr**ow**n, just wash it off!

Page 46

Read this story. Then answer the questions.

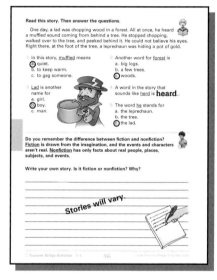

One day, a lad was chopping wood in a forest. All at once, he heard a muffled sound coming from behind a tree. He stopped chopping, walked over to the tree, and peeked behind it. He could not believe his eyes. Right there, at the foot of the tree, a leprechaun was hiding a pot of gold.

1. In this story, muffled means
   a. quiet.
   b. to keep warm.
   c. to gag someone.

2. Another word for forest is
   a. big logs.
   b. a few trees.
   c. woods.

3. Lad is another name for
   a. girl.
   b. boy.
   c. man.

4. A word in the story that sounds like herd is **heard**.

5. The word he stands for
   a. the leprechaun.
   b. the tree.
   c. the lad.

Do you remember the difference between fiction and nonfiction? Fiction is drawn from the imagination, and the events and characters aren't real. Nonfiction has only facts about real people, places, subjects, and events.

Write your own story. Is it fiction or nonfiction? Why?

Stories will vary.

Page 47

Multiplication. Finish the charts.

X2		X3		X4		X5	
4	8	3	9	10	40	9	45
8	16	7	21	5	20	2	10
3	6	2	6	4	16	6	30
6	12	2	6	7	28	5	25
9	18	6	18	3	12	7	35
7	14	8	24	9	36	4	20

Use a word from the box to complete each sentence. Divide the word by what you know about syllables.

trumpet
cottage
circus
pictures
market
quarter
signal
pennies
chatter
curtains

1. I am learning to play the **trum•pet**.
2. Look at all the funny **pic•tures** in this book.
3. You can buy bread and milk at the **mar•ket**.
4. We live in a small **cot•tage**.
5. This pencil costs a **quar•ter**.
6. I am saving lots of **pen•nies** in a jar.
7. The clowns at the **cir•cus** were great.
8. When you hear the **sig•nal**, run fast.
9. We have white **cur•tains** on our window.
10. Chipmunks **chat•ter**.

Page 48

Read the paragraph and answer the questions at the end.

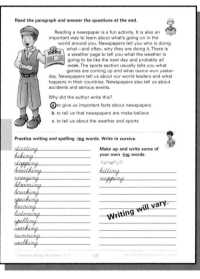

Reading a newspaper is a fun activity. It is also an important way to learn about what's going on in the world around you. Newspapers tell us who is doing what—and often, why they are doing it. There is a weather page to tell you what the weather is going to be like the next day and probably all week. The sports section usually tells us what games are coming up and what teams won yesterday. Newspapers tell us about our world leaders and what happens in their countries. Newspapers also tell us about accidents and serious events.

Why did the author write this?
a. to give us important facts about newspapers
b. to tell us that newspapers are make-believe
c. to tell us about the weather and sports

Practice writing and spelling -ing words. Write in cursive.

starting
hiking
stopping
sneezing
blooming
breaking
speaking
hearing
listening
spelling
working
running
walking

EXAMPLE:
hitting
napping

Make up and write some of your own -ing words.

Writing will vary.

Page 49

Draw a straight line through three numbers that add up to the sum given in each diagram below.

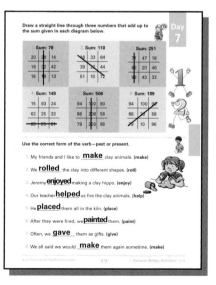

Sum: 78
20	28	14
16	32	42
19	18	13

Sum: 110
24	17	18
39	47	44
51	10	72

Sum: 251
71	47	18
89	20	46
88	43	33

Sum: 149
15	93	24
63	25	33
65	25	61

Sum: 506
94	100	90
88	206	58
79	200	96

Sum: 189
94	100	88
88	58	
10	96	

Use the correct form of the verb—past or present.

1. My friends and I like to **make** clay animals. (make)
2. We **rolled** the clay into different shapes. (roll)
3. Jeremy **enjoyed** making a clay hippo. (enjoy)
4. Our teacher **helped** us fire the clay animals. (help)
5. He **placed** them all in the kiln. (place)
6. After they were fired, we **painted** them. (paint)
7. Often, we **gave** them as gifts. (give)
8. We all said we would **make** them again sometime. (make)

Page 50

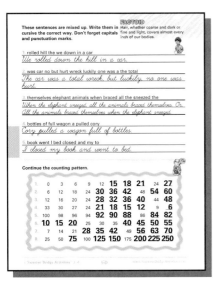

These sentences are mixed up. Write them in cursive the correct way. Don't forget capitals and punctuation marks.

1. rolled hill the we down in a car
We rolled down the hill in a car.
2. was car no but hurt wreck luckily one was a total
The car was a total wreck, but luckily, no one was hurt.
3. themselves elephant animals when braced all the sneezed the
When the elephant sneezed, all the animals braced themselves. Or, All the animals braced themselves when the elephant sneezed.
4. bottles of full wagon a pulled cory
Cory pulled a wagon full of bottles.
5. book went I bed closed and my to
I closed my book and went to bed.

Continue the counting pattern.

1.	0	3	6	9	12	15	18	21	24	27
2.	6	12	18	24	30	36	42	48	54	60
3.	12	16	20	24	28	32	36	40	44	48
4.	33	30	27	24	21	18	15	12	9	6
5.	100	98	96	94	92	90	88	86	84	82
6.	10	15	20	25	30	35	40	45	50	55
7.	7	14	21	28	35	42	49	56	63	70
8.	25	50	75	100	125	150	175	200	225	250

Page 51

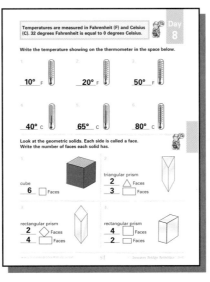

Temperatures are measured in Fahrenheit (F) and Celsius (C). 32 degrees Fahrenheit is equal to 0 degrees Celsius. **Day 8**

Write the temperature showing on the thermometer in the space below.

10° F   20° F   50° F
40° C   65° C   80° C

Look at the geometric solids. Each side is called a face. Write the number of faces each solid has.

cube — 6 Faces
triangular prism — 2 / 3 Faces
rectangular prism — 2 / 4 Faces
rectangular prism — 4 / 2 Faces

Page 52

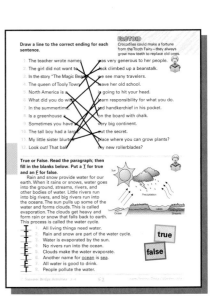

Draw a line to the correct ending for each sentence.
1. The teacher wrote names
2. The girl did not want to
3. In the story "The Magic Beanstalk"
4. The queen of Tooly Town
5. North America is a
6. What did you do with
7. In the summertime,
8. Is a greenhouse
9. Sometimes you have to
10. The tall boy had a large
11. My little sister blurted
12. Look out! That ball

True or False. Read the paragraph; then fill in the blanks below. Put a T for true and an F for false.

Rain and snow provide water for our earth. When it rains or snows, water goes into the ground, streams, rivers, and other bodies of water. Little rivers run into big rivers, and big rivers run into the oceans. The sun pulls up some of the water and forms clouds. This is called evaporation. The clouds get heavy and form rain or snow that falls back to earth. This process is called the water cycle.

T 1. All living things need water.
T 2. Rain and snow are part of the water cycle.
T 3. Water is evaporated by the sun.
F 4. No rivers run into the ocean.
T 5. Clouds make the water evaporate.
F 6. Another name for ocean is sea.
F 7. All water is good to drink.
T 8. People pollute the water.

true   false

Page 53

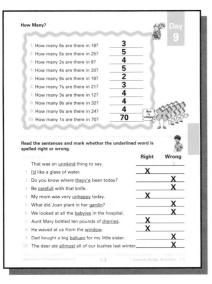

How Many? **Day 9**

1. How many 6s are there in 18? 3
2. How many 5s are there in 25? 5
3. How many 2s are there in 8? 4
4. How many 4s are there in 20? 5
5. How many 9s are there in 18? 2
6. How many 7s are there in 21? 3
7. How many 3s are there in 12? 4
8. How many 8s are there in 32? 4
9. How many 6s are there in 24? 4
10. How many 1s are there in 70? 70

Read the sentences and mark whether the underlined word is spelled right or wrong.

	Right	Wrong
That was an unkind thing to say.	X	
1. I'd like a glass of water.	X	
2. Do you know where they've been today?		X
3. Be carefull with that knife.		X
4. My mom was very unhappy today.	X	
5. What did Joan plant in her gardin?		X
6. We looked at all the babyies in the hospital.		X
7. Aunt Mary bottled ten pounds of cherries.	X	
8. He waved at us from the window.	X	
9. Dad bought a big balluen for my little sister.		X
10. The deer ate allmost all of our bushes last winter.		X

Page 54

Read the story. Write complete sentences for your answers.

Robert and Sydni are two of my very best friends. We have gone to school together since we were in kindergarten. We even go to summer camp and the recreation center together. There are many reasons why I like to be with them. Robert always lets me borrow his skateboard. He knows that if I had a skateboard, I would let him borrow it. Robert is a person you can count on, too. When we are out riding our bikes together, Sydni sometimes has me ride in front while she rides behind me. She understands that the way to be a good friend is by taking turns and being fair.

1. What is it that Robert does to be a good friend?
Robert always lets me borrow his skateboard.
2. Is Sydni a fair person? Why?
Yes, she understands that taking turns is important
3. List three things that the friends do together.
Answers will vary.
4. Write a few sentences of your own about what you think makes a good friend.
Answers will vary.

Page 55

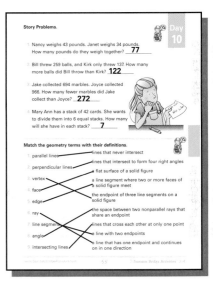

Story Problems. **Day 10**

1. Nancy weighs 43 pounds. Janet weighs 34 pounds. How many pounds do they weigh together? 77
2. Bill threw 259 balls, and Kirk only threw 137. How many more balls did Bill throw than Kirk? 122
3. Jake collected 694 marbles. Joyce collected 966. How many fewer marbles did Jake collect than Joyce? 272
4. Mary Ann has a stack of 42 cards. She wants to divide them into 6 equal stacks. How many will she have in each stack? 7

Match the geometry terms with their definitions.
1. parallel lines — lines that never intersect
2. perpendicular lines — lines that intersect to form four right angles
3. vertex — a flat surface of a solid figure
4. face — a line segment where two or more faces of a solid figure meet
5. edge — the endpoint of three line segments on a solid figure
6. ray — the space between two nonparallel rays that share an endpoint
7. line segment — lines that cross each other at only one point
8. angle — a line with two endpoints
9. intersecting lines — a line that has one endpoint and continues on in one direction

Page 56

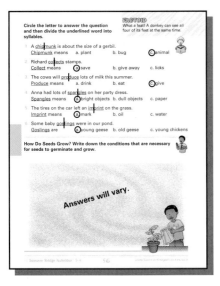

Circle the letter to answer the question and then divide the underlined word into syllables.

1. A chipmunk is about the size of a gerbil. Chipmunk means a. plant b. bug **c. animal**
2. Richard collects stamps. Collect means **a. save** b. give away c. licks
3. The cows will produce lots of milk this summer. Produce means a. drink b. eat **c. give**
4. Anna had lots of spangles on her party dress. Spangles means **a. bright objects** b. dull objects c. paper
5. The tires on the car left an imprint on the grass. Imprint means **a. mark** b. oil c. water
6. Some baby goslings were in our pond. Goslings are **a. young geese** b. old geese c. young chickens

How Do Seeds Grow? Write down the conditions that are necessary for seeds to germinate and grow.
Answers will vary.

Page 57

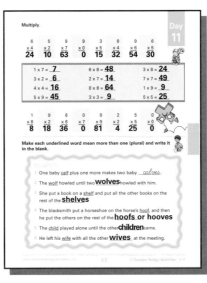

Multiply. **Day 11**

6×4	5×2	9×7	4×0	3×5	8×4	6×9	5×6
24	10	63	0	15	32	54	30

1×7=7   6×8=48   3×8=24
3×2=6   2×7=14   7×7=49
4×4=16   8×8=64   1×9=9
5×9=45   3×3=9   5×5=25

×8	×2	×6	×0	×9	×2	×5	×0
8	18	36	0	81	4	25	0

Make each underlined word mean more than one (plural) and write it in the blank.

1. One baby calf plus one more makes two baby **calves**.
2. The wolf howled until two **wolves** howled with him.
3. She put a book on a shelf and put all the other books on the rest of the **shelves**
4. The blacksmith put a horseshoe on the horse's hoof, and then he put the others on the rest of the **hoofs or hooves**
5. The child played alone until the other **children** came.
6. He left his wife with all the other **wives** at the meeting.

Page 58

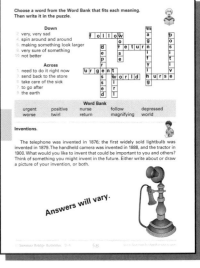

Choose a word from the Word Bank that fits each meaning. Then write it in the puzzle.

Down
1. very, very sad — depressed
2. spin around and around — twirl
3. making something look larger — magnifying
4. very sure of something — positive
5. not better — worse

Across
6. need to do it right now — urgent
7. send back to the store — return
8. take care of the sick — nurse
9. to go after — follow
10. the earth — world

Word Bank: urgent, positive, nurse, follow, depressed, worse, twirl, return, magnifying, world

Inventions.
The telephone was invented in 1876; the first widely sold lightbulb was invented in 1879. The handheld camera was invented in 1888, and the tractor in 1900. What would you like to invent that could be important to you and others? Think of something you might invent in the future. Either write about or draw a picture of your invention, or both.
Answers will vary.

Page 59

Use the graph to answer the questions.

Ms. Fran has many friends. She sends them letters each week. Mark the number of letters she sends each day **on the graph.** (Monday is done for you.) Then answer the questions. Each letter shown stands for four letters.

Mon.
Tues.
Wed.
Thurs.
Fri.

1. How many letters did Ms. Fran send out on Thursday? **20**
2. On what two days did she send out 16 letters? **Tues. and Fri.**
3. What was the fewest she sent in one day? **12**
4. What was the most she sent in one day? **28**

Similarities and Differences. Look at each pair of words. Write down at least one way they are alike and at least one way they are different.

1. leopard and cheetah
2. typewriter and piano

Answers will vary.

3. cabin and tent
4. whistle and sing

Page 60

Slugs have four noses. Watch out when they sneeze!

Real or Make-Believe. Write **M** for make-believe or **R** for real.

R 1. a pumpkin growing on a vine in a field
R 2. a fireman saving a kitten from a tree
M 3. an elephant that can fly in a circus
M 4. a cow that can give chocolate milk
R 5. a family taking a summer vacation
M 6. a chicken that lays golden eggs
R 7. a brother and sister working together
R 8. five children going to a movie in the afternoon
M 9. buckets of paint turning the sky many colors
M 10. a ghost turning a frog into a king
R 11. a tree being blown over by the wind
M 12. a rainbow bridge to the moon

M R

Use the clue to help you fill in the missing letters. Hint: Use vowels.

1. to do something many times — o f t e n
2. a sea animal with eight legs — o ct o p u s
3. a reptile that lives in a swamp — cr o c o d i l e
4. a very small house — c o t a g e
5. something to keep the rain off — u mbr e ll a
6. twelve things — d o z e n
7. a tree or the inner part of your hand — p a lm
8. two things that are different — o pp o s i t e
9. a place that has little rain — d e s e r t
10. you can put this on a Christmas tree — o r n a m e nt
11. a dessert made with eggs — c u st a r d
12. to stop something from happening — pr e v e nt
13. go away — d i s a pp e a r
14. to say you are sorry — a p o l o g i z e

Page 61

Perimeter is the measurement of the length around a figure. You can find the perimeter by adding the lengths of all the sides. Look at the following figures and find the perimeter of each.

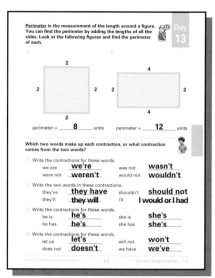

perimeter = **8** units   perimeter = **12** units

Which two words make up each contraction, or what contraction comes from the two words?

1. Write the contractions for these words.

| we are | **we're** | was not | **wasn't** |
| were not | **weren't** | would not | **wouldn't** |

2. Write the two words in these contractions.

| they've | **they have** | shouldn't | **should not** |
| they'll | **they will** | I'd | **I would or I had** |

3. Write the contractions for these words.

| he is | **he's** | she is | **she's** |
| he has | **he's** | she has | **she's** |

4. Write the contractions for these words.

| let us | **let's** | will not | **won't** |
| does not | **doesn't** | we have | **we've** |

Page 62

Your tongue print is as unique as your fingerprint.

Read the directions in the box. Draw a line under the answer to each question.

Instant Oatmeal
1. Empty package into microwaveable bowl.
2. Add 2/3 cup water or milk and stir.
3. Microwave on high 1–2 minutes; stir.
4. Put milk and sugar on top.
5. Eat with a spoon.
6. Clean up.

1. What do the directions tell you how to make?
   a. oatmeal
   b. **instant oatmeal**
   c. cold cereal

2. What is the first step?
   a. turn microwave on
   b. **empty package into bowl**
   c. stir well to mix

3. What things do you need?
   oatmeal package, pan, water or milk, spoon, flour, sugar

4. How long should it take you to make this?
   a. a few seconds b. **a few minutes** c. 30 minutes

Add a prefix to the word after the blank. Use **re-** or **un-**.

1. Please **re** move your shoes before you come in.
2. We will have to **re** build our house.
3. He was very **un** kind to me.
4. I would like to **re** join that club.
5. That was an **un** usual movie.
6. We have to **re** make the cake.
7. Did you feel like you were treated **un** fairly?
8. The children will **re** turn on Saturday.
9. That was an **un** common rainstorm.
10. You will have to **un/re** wrap that gift.

re-   un-

Page 63

Practice finding the differences.

Ex. 5 10
693
– 240
363

300 – 130 = 170
510 – 250 = 260
804 – 163 = 641
435 – 662 = 243
404 – 142 = 262

Ex. 4 9 10
500
– 246
254

623 – 257 = 366
771 – 704 = 77 *(appears as 77)*
900 – 156 = 744
435 – 297 = 138
500 – 297 = 203

Ex. 8 14 10
$9.50
– 6.75
$2.75

$5.00 – 1.62 = $3.38
$6.15 – 4.38 = $1.77
$10.32 – 7.75 = $2.57
$4.06 – 1.67 = $2.39
$1.00 – .67 = $.33

Write, in cursive, a sentence for each of the *-es* words in the box.

hooves
lives
leaves
scarves
wives
wolves

Answers will vary.

Page 64

Most insects must turn their whole bodies to turn their heads—but the praying mantis doesn't need to.

Look at this table of contents and answer the questions.

1. What chapters should you read to learn how to write a story?
   Writing a Story, Communicating with Others

2. On what page would you start reading to learn about commas?
   Page 40

3. How many chapters does this table of contents show? **eight**

4. On which page would you find information on describing what something looks like? **Page 57**

5. Which chapter might tell you how to make a paper airplane?
   Chapter 4 (Following Directions)

Table of Contents
Communicating with Others 9
Writing a Story 16
Word Meanings 20
Following Directions 25
Using Words Correctly 32
Commas 40
Proofreading 53
Describing Words 57

Read the paragraph and add the correct punctuation.

"Where did you go yesterday?" Tanner asked Denise. "I went to the fair," she told him. "I will draw a picture of it for you." She then told him about the watermelon-eating contest and the blue ribbon she won. She told him about seeing pigs and prize-winning sheep. "It sounds like you had a fun day, Denise. I wish I had been with you," said Tanner.

Now draw a picture of something else Denise may have seen at the fair.

Pictures will vary.

Page 65

Read and solve the problems.

1. James planted 5 corn seeds each in 9 holes. How many seeds did he plant?
   5 × 9 = **45**

2. Judy went to a book sale. In 3 days, she bought 24 books. She bought the same number each time she went. How many did she buy each day? 24 ÷ 3 = 8

3. Betty has the same number of nickels as she has dimes. She has $1.80 worth of dimes. How many nickels does she have? **18 nickels**
   She has $ **90** in nickels.

4. Sue babysat four times last week. She made $4 one night, $5.25 on two different nights, and $6.40 on one night. How much did Sue make altogether? **$20.90**

5. There were 95 children on the bus. Ten got off at the first stop. Twenty-two got off at the second stop. How many were left on the bus? **63 children**

6. Allen picked fruit for a farmer last summer. He picked 16 bushels of peaches, 14 bushels of apples, and 18 bushels of pears. How much fruit did Allen pick? **48 bushels**

Write the titles of these books correctly. Remember: the first, last, and all important words need to begin with a capital letter. Write in cursive.

1. nate the great — *Nate the Great*
2. katy and the big snow — *Katy and the Big Snow*
3. claude the dog — *Claude the Dog*
4. emma's dragon hunt — *Emma's Dragon Hunt*
5. the legend of the bluebonnet — *The Legend of the Bluebonnet*
6. the seashore story — *The Seashore Story*
7. soup for the king — *Soup for the King*
8. the storm book — *The Storm Book*

Page 66

Finish writing this story.

The group of hikers did not know how long it had been since anyone had seen Don. "I know he was here just a little while ago," said Fred. Fred had said that two hours ago. There were already search parties out looking for Don.
"Don is a good hiker and should be able to find his way down the mountain," his father was saying. "But maybe he has been hurt," replied Don's friend, Craig.

Stories will vary.

Try making a comparison with nature or something else.

EXAMPLE: The first daffodils were as yellow as *lemons*.

1. The piano keys were as white as _____.
2. That horse is as black as a dark _____.
3. The fireworks were as bright as the _____.
4. Her eyes were as green as the _____.
5. That house was as tall as a steep _____.
6. The balloons reminded me of a bunch of _____.
7. The mud between my toes was as brown as _____.
8. The sunset was as red and orange as _____.
9. The rings on her fingers sparkled like _____.
10. The wind was as gentle as _____.
11. The new leaves on the trees in spring are as green as _____.
12. My new sweater was as blue as the summer _____.

Answers will vary.

Page 67

Count the money.

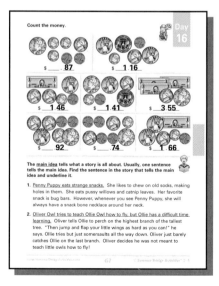

$. 87 $ 1 . 16

$ 1 . 46 $ 1 . 41 $ 3 . 55

$. 92 $. 74 $ 1 . 66

The **main idea** tells what a story is all about. Usually, one sentence tells the main idea. Find the sentence in the story that tells the main idea and underline it.

1. Penny Puppy eats strange snacks. She likes to chew on old socks, making holes in them. She eats pussy willows and catnip leaves. Her favorite snack is bug bars. However, whenever you see Penny Puppy, she will always have a snack bone necklace around her neck.

2. Oliver Owl tries to teach Ollie Owl how to fly, but Ollie has a difficult time learning. Oliver tells Ollie to perch on the highest branch of the tallest tree. "Then jump and flap your little wings as hard as you can!" he says. Ollie tries but just somersaults all the way down. Oliver just barely catches Ollie on the last branch. Oliver decides he was not meant to teach little owls how to fly!

Page 68

Write a story about the picture. Be sure to use capital letters and periods where needed. Give your story a title.

FACTOID
Ball lightning is tricky—it can float right through glass or smash the glass to smithereens!

Things to think about:
Who is the story about?
Where does the story take place?
How does this story begin?
What happens next?
How will this story end?

Stories will vary.

Page 69

Day 17

Use the information given on meters and kilometers to help you solve the problems.

1 meter = 100 centimeters   1 kilometer = 1,000 meters
cm = centimeter   m = meter   km = kilometer

Choose a unit so the answers seem reasonable.

1. Randy is 150 **cm** tall.
2. Jane's room is 5 **m** wide.
3. Whitney's hand is 14 **cm** long and 5 **cm** wide.
4. The distance from Florida to Texas is 1,150 **km**.
5. The flagpole at the post office is 46 **m** tall.
6. I can touch the wall 163 **cm** high.
7. Mr. Hobbs drove his car 84 **km** the first hour.
8. Joyce's room is about 6 **m** wide.
9. Jack and Jill walked approximately 3 **km** in 30 minutes.

Writers sometimes use words that stand for other words. They call them word referents. Read each sentence. Circle the word that the underlined word stands for.
EXAMPLE:

1. Betty has a (computer.) She keeps it on her desk.
2. (Dora) said, "I have to go home now to visit my grandmother."
3. Bill asked (Juan) if he was going to play baseball this year.
4. (Jack and Jean) both collect seashells. Sometimes they trade with one another.
5. (Rachel) plays the violin, and sometimes she sings, too.
6. When the big, gray (dog) saw the cat, it barked and growled.
7. Our (school bus) is always crowded, and it is usually very noisy, too.
8. (Mom) might let us go sledding today. We might get her to drive us to the hill at the park.

Page 70

Read the story and answer the questions.

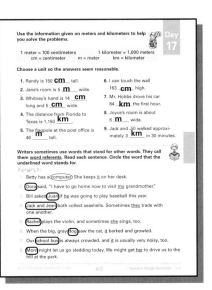

Denise has a dog named Pocket. Pocket hates to take a bath. Whenever he hears water running, Pocket runs outside and hides in the playhouse. Last week, Denise decided Pocket had to have a bath. Denise took a round tub out on the lawn and started to fill it with warm water. When the tub was ready, Denise called her dog. "Come here, Pocket. It's time for your bath."

1. Do you think Pocket will come to Denise? Why or why not?

2. Where do you think Denise will find him? Why?

Answers will vary.

3. What would you do if you had a dog like Pocket?

Read the paragraph and answer the questions.

The children were playing baseball in the empty lot. Peggy was at bat. She swung hard and hit the ball farther than anyone else had. The ball sailed across the lot and smashed through Mrs. Allen's window. Peggy knew Mrs. Allen would be really angry. The other kids scattered, running for home. Peggy looked at the broken window.

1. What do you think Peggy will do?

2. Which clues help you to decide?

Answers will vary.

Page 71

Day 18

Find the missing factors. One factor and the product are given to you.

1. **2** x 3 = 6   **5** x 6 = 30   4 x **4** = 16
2. 3 x **6** = 18   7 x **2** = 14   **2** x 9 = 18
3. 1 x **5** = 5   12 x **1** = 12   **3** x 8 = 24
4. 1 x **9** = 9   4 x **7** = 28   9 x **9** = 81
5. 3 x **7** = 21   **5** x 5 = 25   **7** x 7 = 49
6. 2 x **2** = 4   4 x **9** = 36   8 x **9** = 72
7. 5 x **9** = 45   2 x **15** = 30   10 x **5** = 50
8. 12 x **3** = 36   3 x **9** = 27   6 x **10** = 60

The words in each row go together in some way. Write two more words to go with them.

1. robin, owl, pigeon   *quail*   *pheasant*
2. peaches, apples, pears
3. spoon, bowl, cup
4. lake, pond, river
5. branch, sticks, wood   *Answers will vary.*
6. lemonade, water, milk
7. dollar, dime, penny
8. carrot, celery, pears
9. dress, shoes, skirt
10. tennis, golf, racquetball

Page 72

Day 18

Fill in the blanks using these words: plant, heat, sunlight, plants. Earth, sunlight, oxygen. Then answer the questions below.

FACTOID
Glass isn't actually a solid—it's a liquid that moves very, very, very slowly.

Sunlight is very important to our planet, **Earth**. It provides us with food, oxygen, and heat. Most of our food comes from **plant** life. **Plants** also give off the **oxygen** we breathe. Without **sunlight** plants would die, and we would not have food or air. The **sunlight** also heats the earth. Without it, we would freeze to death.

1. What is the topic?
   a. food
   (b) sunlight
   c. oxygen
   d. plants

2. What is the main idea?
   (a) Sunlight is important to the earth.
   b. Sunlight heats plants.
   c. People would freeze without sunlight.
   d. Sunlight hurts your eyes.

Words that mean about the same thing are called synonyms. Write, in cursive, a synonym from the box below for the word listed.

EX easy	*simple*	shout	*yell*	change	*alter*
also	*too*	jacket	*coat*	home	*house*
gift	*present*	car	*automobile*	complete	*finish*
close	*shut*	gem	*jewel*	join	*connect*
shy	*timid*	penny	*cent*	mistake	*error*
wet	*moist*	rug	*carpet*	argument	*dispute*
rich	*wealthy*	couch	*sofa*	scared	*afraid*

simple   yell   present   timid   house   shut   afraid
finish   jewel   sofa   coat   error   automobile   moist
too   carpet   wealthy   alter   cent   connect   dispute

Page 73

Day 19

Mixed Skill Practice.

12	8	15	6	13	14
− 8	+ 9	x 4	− 9	x 7	− 5	+ 7
4	**17**	**24**	**6**	**42**	**8**	**21**

19	46	75	38	44	83	57
+ 39	− 28	− 39	+ 17	− 15	− 47	+ 34
58	**18**	**36**	**55**	**29**	**36**	**91**

8	4	3	27	40	35	65
x 4	x 7	x 9	+ 19	− 8	+ 44	− 59
32	**28**	**27**	**46**	**32**	**79**	**6**

804	132	176	921	608	304	657
− 238	− 78	+ 394	+ 496	− 239	− 127	− 589
566	**54**	**570**	**1,417**	**369**	**177**	**68**

Pretend you were walking in a park last night and saw a spaceship land. Write a paragraph about it. How did it look? How did it make you feel? Did anyone else see it? Did you see or speak to anyone or anything?

Answers will vary.

Page 74

Divide the shapes according to the fraction asked for.
EXAMPLE:

1. thirds   2. fourths   3. fifths
4. eighths   5. halves   6. tenths
7. sixths   8. ninths   9. sevenths

10. Start with a paper strip ▭ Fold it once. Fold it again. Fold it once more. Before you unfold it, think to yourself, "How do the folds divide the paper, and how many equal parts do I have?" Now check to see if you are right.

Write the words under the correct word category.

buttermilk
airplane
snowstorm
selection
replanted
overweight
sleepless
peaceful
happiness
football
daylight
unpacked

Compound words	Words with prefixes or suffixes
buttermilk	**selection**
airplane	**replanted**
snowstorm	**sleepless**
overweight	**peaceful**
football	**happiness**
daylight	**unpacked**

Page 75

Day 20

Read the story carefully. Watch for word meanings.

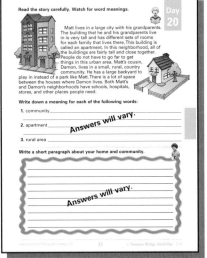

Matt lives in a large city with his grandparents. The building that he and his grandparents live in is very tall and has different sets of rooms for each family that lives there. This building is called an apartment. In this neighborhood, all of the buildings are fairly tall and close together. People do not have to go far to get things in this urban area. Matt's cousin, Damon, lives in a small, rural, country community. He has a large backyard to play in instead of a park like Matt. There is a lot of space between the houses where Damon lives. Both Matt's and Damon's neighborhoods have schools, hospitals, stores, and other places people need.

Write down a meaning for each of the following words:

1. community

2. apartment   *Answers will vary.*

3. rural area

Write a short paragraph about your home and community.

Answers will vary.

Page 76

It's Time Again!

FACTOID
What a bird brain! An ostrich's eye is bigger than its brain.

1. Write the times.

6:15   **12:45**   **10:43**   **9:22**

2. Look at the clock below and answer the questions.
   What time does the clock show?   **5:45**
   What time would it have been 15 minutes earlier?   **5:30**
   What time will it be in half an hour?   **6:15**
   Can you think of a way to write the time other than the way you wrote it before? *Answers will vary.*
   What time would it show if you switched the hands?   **9:28**

Find the correctly spelled word. Circle it; then write it in the blank to complete the sentence.

1. Astronauts are **weightless** while they are in space.
   waitless   (weightless)   waghtless   wateless

2. The **thoughtful** children picked up litter along the streets.
   thotful   toughtful   (thoughtful)   thowghtful

3. The **neighborly** woman invited the new family for dinner.
   (neighborly)   neighborlie   naborly   knaborly

4. We need to remember to keep our doctor's **appointment**.
   apointment   apowntment   (appointment)

5. Make some **copies** of this, please.
   copyes   (copies)   copeis   coppies

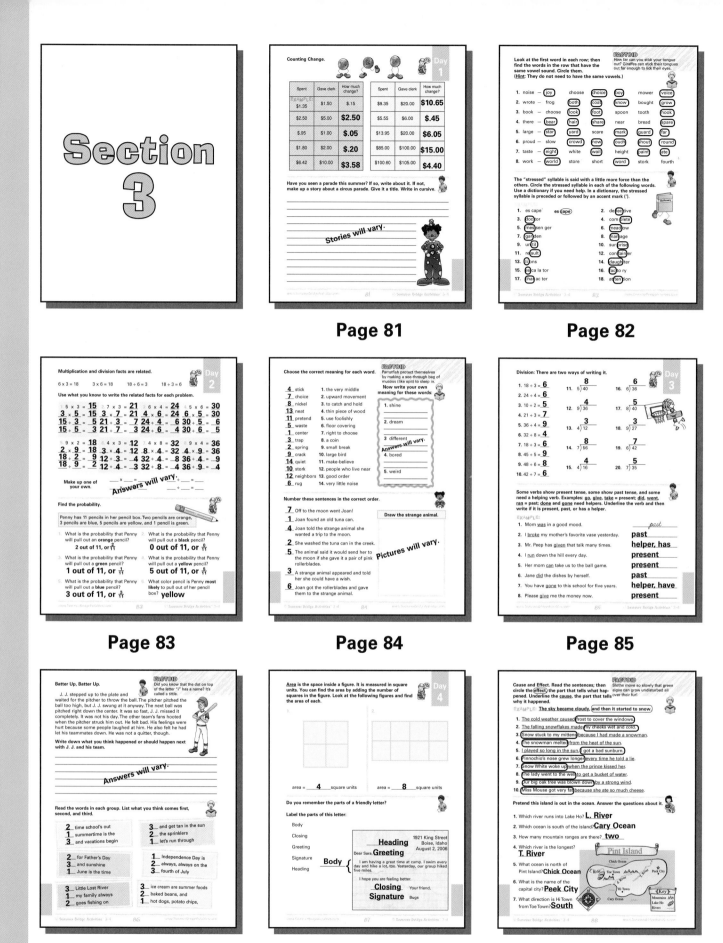

Section 3

Page 81

Counting Change.

Spent	Gave clerk	How much change?		Spent	Gave clerk	How much change?
EXAMPLE: $1.35	$1.50	$.15		$9.35	$20.00	$10.65
$2.50	$5.00	$2.50		$5.55	$6.00	$.45
$.95	$1.00	$.05		$13.95	$20.00	$6.05
$1.80	$2.00	$.20		$85.00	$100.00	$15.00
$6.42	$10.00	$3.58		$100.60	$105.00	$4.40

Have you seen a parade this summer? If so, write about it. If not, make up a story about a circus parade. Give it a title. Write in cursive.

Stories will vary.

Page 82

Look at the first word in each row; then find the words in the row that have the same vowel sound. Circle them. (Hint: They do not need to have the same vowels.)

1. noise — joy, choice, boy, voice
2. wrote — both, coat, know, grow
3. book — look, foot, hook
4. there — bear, hair, share, spare
5. large — star, yard, mark, guard, far
6. proud — crowd, now, ouch, shout
7. taste — eight, wait, paint, ate
8. work — world, word, stork

Circle the stressed syllable in each of the following words.

1. es·cape' / es·cape
3. doc·tor
5. mes·sen·ger
9. un·til
11. re·sult
13. li·ons
15. es·ca·la·tor
17. char·ac·ter
2. com·plete
4. de·tec·tive
6. mead·ow
8. man·age
10. sur·prise
12. con·tain·er
14. daugh·ter
16. fac·to·ry
18. at·ten·tion

Page 83

Multiplication and division facts are related.

5 x 3 = 15, 3 x 5 = 21, 4 x 6 = 24, 6 x 5 = 30
3 ÷ 5 = 15, 3 ÷ 7 = 21, 4 ÷ 6 = 24, 6 ÷ 5 = 30
15 ÷ 3 = 21, 7 ÷ 3 = 24, 4 ÷ 6 = 30, 6 ÷ 5 = 5
15 ÷ 5 = 21, 7 ÷ 3 = 24, 6 ÷ 4 = 30, 6 ÷ 5 = 5

9 x 2 = 18, 4 x 3 = 12, 4 x 8 = 32, 9 x 4 = 36
2 ÷ 9 = 18, 3 ÷ 4 = 12, 8 ÷ 4 = 32, 4 ÷ 9 = 36
18 ÷ 2 = 9, 12 ÷ 3 = 4, 32 ÷ 4 = 8, 36 ÷ 9 = 4
18 ÷ 9 = 2, 12 ÷ 4 = 3, 32 ÷ 8 = 4, 36 ÷ 9 = 4

Answers will vary.

Find the probability.

Penny has 11 pencils in her pencil box. Two pencils are orange, 3 pencils are blue, 5 pencils are yellow, and 1 pencil is green.

1. orange pencil? **2 out of 11, or 2/11**
2. black pencil? **0 out of 11, or 0/11**
3. green pencil? **1 out of 11, or 1/11**
4. yellow pencil? **5 out of 11, or 5/11**
5. blue pencil? **3 out of 11, or 3/11**
6. most likely? **yellow**

Page 84

Choose the correct meaning for each word.

4 stick — 1. the very middle
7 choice — 2. upward movement
8 nickel — 3. to catch and hold
13 neat — 4. thin piece of wood
11 pretend — 5. use foolishly
5 waste — 6. floor covering
1 center — 7. right to choose
3 trap — 8. a coin
2 spring — 9. small break
9 crack — 10. large bird
14 quiet — 11. make-believe
10 stork — 12. people who live near
12 neighbors — 13. good order
6 rug — 14. very little noise

Now write your own meaning for these words: *Answers will vary.*
1. shine
2. dream
3. different
4. bored
5. weird

Number these sentences in the correct order.
7 Off to the moon went Joan!
1 Joan found an old tuna can.
4 Joan told the strange animal she wanted a trip to the moon.
2 She washed the tuna can in the creek.
5 The animal said it would send her to the moon if she gave it a pair of pink rollerblades.
3 A strange animal appeared and told her she could have a wish.
6 Joan got the rollerblades and gave them to the strange animal.

Draw the strange animal. *Pictures will vary.*

Page 85

Division: There are two ways of writing it.

1. 18 ÷ 3 = 6
2. 24 ÷ 4 = 6
3. 10 ÷ 2 = 5
4. 21 ÷ 3 = 7
5. 36 ÷ 4 = 9
6. 32 ÷ 8 = 4
7. 18 ÷ 3 = 6
8. 45 ÷ 5 = 9
9. 48 ÷ 6 = 8
10. 42 ÷ 7 = 6
11. 5)40 = 8
12. 9)36 = 4
13. 4)12 = 3
14. 7)56 = 8
15. 4)16 = 4
16. 6)36 = 6
17. 5)40 = 8
18. 9)27 = 3
19. 7)42 = 6
20. 7)35 = 5

Underline the verb and then write if it is present, past, or has a helper.

1. Mom was in a good mood. — past
2. I broke my mother's favorite vase yesterday. — past
3. Mr. Peep had given that talk many times. — helper, has
4. I run down the hill every day. — present
5. Her mom can take us to the ball game. — present
6. Jane did the dishes by herself. — past
7. You have gone to this school for five years. — helper, have
8. Please give me the money now. — present

Page 86

Batter Up, Batter Up.

Write down what you think happened or should happen next with J. J. and his team. *Answers will vary.*

Read the words in each group. List what you think comes first, second, and third.

2 time school's out
1 summertime is the
3 and vacations begin

3 and get tan in the sun
2 the sprinklers
1 let's run through

2 for Father's Day
3 and sunshine
1 June is the time

1 Independence Day is
2 always, always on the
3 fourth of July

3 Little Lost River
1 my family always
2 goes fishing on

3 ice cream are summer foods
2 baked beans, and
1 hot dogs, potato chips,

Page 87

Area is the space inside a figure.

area = **4** square units
area = **8** square units

Label the parts of this letter:
Heading, Greeting, Body, Closing, Signature

1921 King Street
Boise, Idaho
August 2, 2006

Dear Sara,

I am having a great time at camp. I swim every day and hike a lot, too. Yesterday, our group hiked five miles.

I hope you are feeling better.

Your friend,
Bugs

Page 88

Cause and Effect. Read the sentences; then circle the effect. Underline the cause.

EXAMPLE: The sky became cloudy, and then it started to snow.

1. The cold weather caused frost to cover the windows.
2. The falling snowflakes made my cheeks wet and cold.
3. Snow stuck to my mittens because I had made a snowman.
4. The snowman melted from the heat of the sun.
5. I played so long in the sun, I got a bad sunburn.
6. Pinocchio's nose grew longer every time he told a lie.
7. Snow White woke up when the prince kissed her.
8. Our lady went to the well to get a bucket of water.
9. Our big oak tree was blown down by a strong wind.
10. Miss Mouse got very fat because she ate so much cheese.

Pretend this island is out in the ocean. Answer the questions about it.

1. Which river runs into Lake Ho? **L. River**
2. Which ocean is south of the island? **Cary Ocean**
3. How many mountain ranges are there? **two**
4. Which river is the longest? **T. River**
5. What ocean is north of Pint Island? **Chick Ocean**
6. What is the name of the capital city? **Peek City**
7. What direction is Hi Town from Toe Town? **South**

Page 89

Division.

$\frac{8}{7)56}$ $\frac{4}{7)28}$ $\frac{4}{8)32}$ $\frac{6}{8)48}$

$\frac{9}{6)54}$ $\frac{7}{5)35}$ $\frac{7}{7)42}$ $\frac{5}{9)45}$

$\frac{3}{6)18}$ $\frac{7}{7)49}$ $\frac{9}{9)81}$ $\frac{6}{6)36}$

$24 ÷ 6 = 4$ $63 ÷ 7 = 9$ $25 ÷ 5 = 5$

$12 ÷ 4 = 3$ $72 ÷ 9 = 8$ $28 ÷ 7 = 4$

Circle the pronouns in the sentences. Remember: A pronoun takes the place of a noun. There can be more than one in some sentences.

1. I told her about Val's horse.
2. This piece of cake is for him.
3. Liz invited Joe and me to the party.
4. The table is all set for us.
5. We are too late to see the first show.
6. They will be happy to come with us.
7. Ray caught two bugs, and later he freed them.
8. This pie is for you and me to eat for dessert.
9. Lisa had a hard time doing the test, but it is over now.
10. Clams and turtles have shells. They are protected by them.
11. He is Jan's best friend.
12. They have been best friends for a long time.

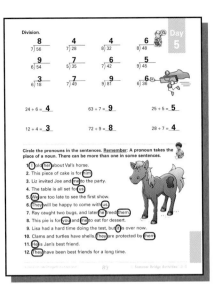

Page 90

Unscramble the words and write them correctly to complete the sentences.

FACTOID
Sneezes can travel out of your mouth at speeds over 100 m.p.h! Now that's speedy!

1. Pillows are to soft as boards are to **hard** — rdha
2. Oranges are to juicy as crackers are to **dry** — dyr
3. Braces are to teeth as glasses are to **eyes** — esey
4. Bells are to ring as cars are to **honk** — nkho
5. Hear is to ears as touch is to **fingers** — serinfg
6. Shout is to noise as whisper is to **quiet** — uetqi
7. Star is to pointed as circle is to **round** — dunor
8. Scaly is to fish as furry is to **kitten** — ttnike
9. Ant is to crawl as frog is to **leap** — pael
10. Elephant is to large as mouse is to **small** — malsl
11. Paint is to brush as draw is to **pencil** — cienlp
12. Buckle is to belt as tie is to **shoelace** — lacehos

Think of a story to fit the pictures. Write in the words.

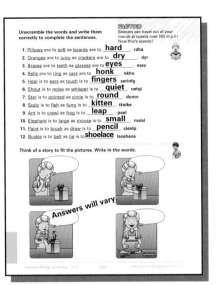

Answers will vary.

Page 91

Adding more than two addends.

65	22	78	51	42	87
59	46	32	26	39	32
+ 11	+ 38	+ 21	+ 26	+ 71	+ 19
135	**106**	**131**	**103**	**152**	**138**

54	38	39	43	37	17
19	22	71	36	46	19
+ 68	+ 46	+ 42	+ 18	+ 28	+ 12
141	**106**	**152**	**97**	**111**	**48**

215	325	429	742	395	
463	48	330	135	205	
+ 306	+ 113	+ 127	+ 173	+ 341	
984	**486**	**886**	**1,050**	**941**	

Read the following words. Write down how many vowels are in each word, how many vowel sounds you hear, and how many syllables there are.

EXAMPLE: afraid

v	vs	syl
3	2	2

	v	vs	syl			v	vs	syl
1. afternoon	4	3	3	8. education	5	4	4
2. formula	3	3	3	9. problem	2	2	2
3. separated	4	4	4	10. migrate	3	2	2
4. fantastic	3	3	3	11. submarine	4	3	3
5. memories	4	3	3	12. belated	3	3	3
6. experience	5	4	4	13. advertising	4	4	4
7. successful	3	3	3	14. characteristic	5	5	5

Page 92

Write your own ending for each sentence. Try to use more than two or three words. Write in cursive.

FACTOID
How long is a "jiffy," anyway? Actually, it's 1/100th of a second!

1. I like the flavor of _____
2. My parents disapproved when I _____
3. I once read a story about a boy who became a knight because he _____
4. The rodeo started with _____
5. Richard swam over to the dock to _____
6. The kite drifted away _____
7. The baby crawled across _____
8. The long winter was beginning _____
9. Lance won a prize for _____
10. Do you like to play _____

Answers will vary.

Can you put these puzzle pieces together and read the message? Don't cut them out. If you need more help, trace the pieces and practice on a sheet of scratch paper. The c and the m are already there to help you.

I WOULD
LIKE TO
BECOME
FAMOUS
AND USE
WISDOM

Page 93

Find the products.

EXAMPLE:
$\frac{2}{\begin{array}{r}58\\ \times 3\\ \hline 174\end{array}}$

42 ×8 = **336**	67 ×5 = **335**	66 ×3 = **198**	35 ×6 = **210**	23 ×3 = **69**
23 ×9 = **207**	29 ×4 = **116**	25 ×9 = **225**	44 ×6 = **264**	94 ×2 = **188**	35 ×8 = **280**
25 ×4 = **100**	21 ×6 = **126**	75 ×4 = **300**	68 ×3 = **204**	41 ×7 = **287**	63 ×2 = **126**

A pronoun showing ownership is a possessive pronoun, such as…

mine   ours   your   his   hers   their   its   my   our

Write six sentences in cursive. Use a possessive pronoun in each one of them.

Answers will vary.

Page 94

What does the underlined phrase really mean? Circle your answer.

FACTOID
The lungfish can live out of the water for about four years—but it tries to stay in the water when it can.

1. It was raining cats and dogs.
   a. Real cats and dogs were falling out of the sky.
   b. It was raining very hard.
   c. It wasn't raining at all.

2. The night was black as coal.
   a. The night was very dark.
   b. The sky was light.
   c. The night was turning into day.

3. I was so thirsty I felt like I could spit cotton.
   a. My mouth was very dry.
   b. I had cotton in my mouth.
   c. I did not need a drink.

4. The sun on the snow made it sparkle like diamonds.
   a. There were diamonds in the snow.
   b. The snow was dirty and dull.
   c. The snow was clean and shiny.

5. Time flies when we are having fun.
   a. Time goes quickly.
   b. Time has wings and flies like a bird.
   c. Time goes slowly.

6. The train roared like a lion as it went through the mountain pass.
   a. The train was quiet.
   b. The train has a voice.
   c. The train was loud and fast.

7. My sister is as gentle as a lamb with sick people.
   a. My sister is soft.
   b. My sister doesn't like sick people.
   c. My sister is kind to sick people.

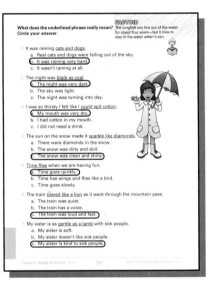

Page 95

Find the quotients and the remainders.

EXAMPLE:
$\frac{6 R2}{4)26}$

$\frac{4R2}{3)14}$ $\frac{7R4}{5)39}$ $\frac{5R1}{5)16}$

$\frac{9R1}{2)19}$ $\frac{4R5}{6)29}$ $\frac{5R1}{4)21}$ $\frac{7R1}{5)36}$

$\frac{6R4}{5)34}$ $\frac{5R2}{7)37}$ $\frac{8R2}{5)42}$ $\frac{8R1}{4)33}$

$\frac{42}{2)84}$ $\frac{20}{3)60}$ $\frac{17}{3)51}$ $\frac{24}{4)96}$

Cursive writing review. School starts soon, so remember to…

1. Make each letter smooth and clear.
2. Space letters evenly.
3. Make each letter the correct shape and size.
4. Make each letter touch the line correctly.
5. Make your letters slant in the same direction.

Copy the following statement, or do one of your own!

I love to practice writing in cursive. It makes me feel very grown-up!

Answers will vary.

Page 96

Get a dictionary. Look up the following words and write the special spelling for each word in the blank provided. Put in all the markings.

FACTOID
People once believed that the vein in the left ring finger (the wedding ring finger) went directly to the heart.

EXAMPLE:
magnolia mag nōl′ yə

Remember: The special spelling tells you how to say a word correctly, how many syllables there are, where they are divided, and which syllable is stressed.

1. porcupine pôr′-kyə -pīn′
2. cupboard kŭb′ ərd
3. electromagnet -lěk′ trō-mǎg′nĭ t
4. chisel chĭ z′ əl
5. elate ĭ -lāt′
6. testify těs′ t ə -fī′
7. gravity grǎv′-ĭ -tē
8. nitrate nī′ trāt′

Choose three words from above and write their meanings.

1. word _____ meaning _____
2. word _____ meaning _____
3. word _____ meaning _____

Answers will vary.

We taste things because of our tongue and nose. The smell helps our tongue taste things. Ask your parents if you can taste some foods you have in your house. Tell whether they are bitter, sour, sweet, or salty. Write the name of the food you tasted under the correct heading.

EXAMPLE:

Bitter	Sour	Sweet	Salty
	lemon		

Answers will vary.

Page 97

Complete the times table wheels.

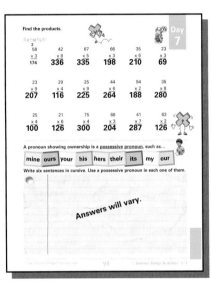

Underline the base, or root, word in each word.

blossoms	immediately	wreckage	incorrect
misspelled	inspector	retrace	reappear
exporting	invention	exhausted	messages

Underline the prefix in each word.

unusual	microphone	submarine	disappoint
displeased	invisible	extend	misplace
defrost	encircle	recover	enlarge

Underline the suffix in each word.

happiness	silently	tiniest	potatoes
hesitated	pleasantly	hasty	scarcely
mouthful	careless	graceful	spelling

Page 98

Read each sentence. Put an <u>F</u> in the blank if the sentence is a fact. Write an <u>O</u> if it is an opinion. The first one has been done for you.

EXAMPLE!

1. Christmas is always on the 25th of December. ___F___
2. Springtime is everyone's favorite time of year. ___O___
3. Birthdays are always a fun day for everyone. ___O___
4. Daylight and nighttime depend on the sun. ___F___
5. Dogs are said to be a man's best friend. ___O___
6. A spaceship travels faster than any airplane. ___F___
7. Lava rock was once a hot liquid. ___F___
8. Eating too much candy is hard on your teeth. ___F___
9. Most children like hot dogs and ice cream. ___O___
10. Reading is one of the most important things in our lives. ___O___

Making Comparisons. Cut an apple in half, draw a picture of it, and label the parts. Draw a picture of the earth. Pretend that you cut a section out. Label its parts.

Apple	Earth
Drawings will vary.	Drawings will vary.

1. How is the apple similar to the inside of the earth?
Answers will vary.

2. How is the apple different from the inside of the earth?
Answers will vary.

Page 99

Match the division and multiplication problems that are related.

EXAMPLE:

12 ÷ 4	5 x 5	38 ÷ 2	43 x 5
16 ÷ 4	3 x 4	63 ÷ 3	22 x 4
15 ÷ 5	6 x 4	50 ÷ 2	49 x 2
24 ÷ 6	4 x 5	84 ÷ 4	21 x 3
36 ÷ 9	9 x 5	56 ÷ 4	43 x 2
45 ÷ 9	7 x 4	88 ÷ 4	29 x 2
20 ÷ 5	2 x 8	86 ÷ 2	25 x 2
64 ÷ 8	5 x 4	80 ÷ 5	44 x 4
25 ÷ 9	3 x 9	58 ÷ 2	16 x 3
81 ÷ 9	8 x 9	51 ÷ 3	47 x 3
72 ÷ 9	9 x 9	86 ÷ 2	48 x 4

Look at the first word in each row. Circle the other words in the row that have the same vowel sound. Write a word of your own to go with the others with the same vowel sound.

Answers will vary.

1. team — (treat) (chief) earth (sheep)
2. toast — (bowl) cow (both) (though)
3. group — (truth) jump (cool) (troop)
4. roll — (boat) (stole) pool (told)
5. scoop — (droop) (juice) (soup) cook
6. yawn — (jaws) chose salt (lawn)
7. twice — (died) (buy) since (price)
8. third — (church) torn (earth) (fern)

Page 100

Can you put the words in these mixed-up sentences in order to make sense?

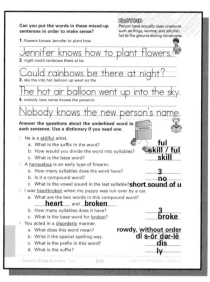

FACTOID
People have actually seen creatures such as frogs, worms, and jellyfish fall to the ground during rainstorms.

1. flowers knows Jennifer to plant how
<u>Jennifer knows how to plant flowers.</u>

2. night could rainbows there at be
<u>Could rainbows be there at night?</u>

3. sky into hot balloon up went air the
<u>The hot air balloon went up into the sky.</u>

4. nobody name new knows the person's
<u>Nobody knows the new person's name.</u>

Answer the questions about the underlined word in each sentence. Use a dictionary if you need one.

1. He is a skillful artist.
a. What is the suffix in the word? **ful / ful**
b. How would you divide the word into syllables? **skill**
c. What is the base word? **skill**

2. A harquebus is an early type of firearm.
a. How many syllables does the word have? **3**
b. Is it a compound word? **no**
c. What is the vowel sound in the last syllable? **short sound of u**

3. I was heartbroken when my puppy was run over by a car.
a. What are the two words in this compound word? **heart** and **broken**
b. How many syllables does it have? **3**
c. What is the base word for broken? **broke**

4. You acted in a disorderly manner.
a. What does this word mean? **rowdy, without order**
b. Write it the special spelling way. **dĭ s-ôr'dər-lē**
c. What is the prefix in this word? **dis**
d. What is the suffix? **ly**

Page 101

Estimate. Circle the answer you think best.

1. A bathtub would hold (10 quarts or (10 gallons) of water.
2. A flower vase would hold (1 pint) or 1 gallon) of water.
3. A fishbowl would hold (3 quarts) or 3 cups) of water.
4. A big glass would hold (1 pint) or 1 quart) of milk.
5. A bicycle would weigh (20 ounces or (20 pounds)
6. An orange would weigh (7 ounces) or 7 pounds.
7. A new pencil would weigh (1 ounce) or 1 pound.
8. A cob of corn would be (11 inches) or 11 yards) long.
9. A new pencil would be (7 inches) or 7 yards) long.
10. A person could read a 1,500-page book in (16 minutes or (6 hours)

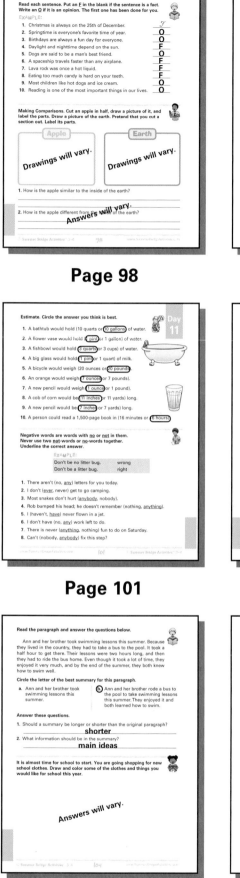

Negative words are words with <u>no</u> or <u>not</u> in them. Never use two <u>not</u>-words or <u>no</u>-words together. Underline the correct answer.

EXAMPLE:

| Don't be no litter bug. | wrong |
| Don't be a litter bug. | right |

1. There aren't (no, <u>any</u>) letters for you today.
2. I don't (<u>ever</u>, never) get to go camping.
3. Most snakes don't hurt (<u>anybody</u>, nobody).
4. Rob bumped his head; he doesn't remember (nothing, <u>anything</u>).
5. I (haven't, <u>have</u>) never flown in a jet.
6. I don't have (no, <u>any</u>) work left to do.
7. There is never (<u>anything</u>, nothing) fun to do on Saturday.
8. Can't (nobody, <u>anybody</u>) fix this step?

Page 102

Read this story and answer the questions by drawing your own conclusions.

Julie Ann and Clint closed their eyes to shut out the sun's glare. As they lay on the ground, the hot July sun felt good. They could hear the wind blowing ever so softly through the pine trees, making a kind of whispering, murmuring sound. They could hear the creek nearby making soothing, babbling sounds. They could even hear the distant screech of a hawk flying high in the sky overhead.

1. Where do you think they are? **Answers will vary.**
2. What season of the year is it? **summer**
3. What other creatures do you think could be there? **Answers will vary.**
4. What would you like to do if you were there? **Answers will vary.**

Design a funny or clever birthday party invitation.

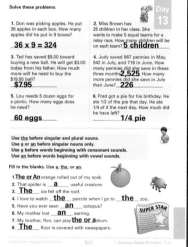

Answers will vary.

Page 103

Find the sums.

246	500	924	402	550
+ 129	+ 806	+ 289	+ 629	+ 758
375	**1,306**	**1,213**	**1,031**	**1,308**

1,284	7,762	3,383	4,290	4,006
+ 2,629	+ 1,473	+ 5,007	+ 2,968	+ 6,974
3,913	**9,235**	**8,390**	**7,258**	**10,980**

9,542	2,423	3,252	6,666	1,920
+ 695	+ 1,932	+ 4,008	+ 4,208	+ 1,940
10,237	**4,355**	**7,260**	**10,874**	**3,860**

An adjective is a word that describes a noun. Fill in the blanks with adjectives.

EXAMPLE:

1. The bathroom is **red**.
2. A _____ family moved in next door yesterday.
3. The bear has _____ fur.
4. The _____ woke me up this morning.
5. Her _____ _____ balloon floated away.

Answers will vary.

Some adjectives tell which one. Use this and that with singular nouns, these and those with plural nouns.

1. Those or these kittens are making too much noise.
2. This or that book is too long for me to read.
3. Is this or that one the hat Mom wanted?
4. **That** planet is very far away.
5. **Those** ducks didn't come back to the pond this year.

Page 104

Read the paragraph and answer the questions below.

Ann and her brother took swimming lessons this summer. Because they lived in the country, they had to take a bus to the pool. It took a half hour to get there. Their lessons were two hours long, and then they had to ride the bus home. Even though it took a lot of time, they enjoyed it very much, and by the end of the summer, they both knew how to swim well.

Circle the letter of the best summary for this paragraph.

a. Ann and her brother took swimming lessons this summer.

(b.) Ann and her brother rode a bus to the pool to take swimming lessons this summer. They enjoyed it and both learned how to swim.

Answer these questions.

1. Should a summary be longer or shorter than the original paragraph?
shorter

2. What information should be in the summary?
main ideas

It is almost time for school to start. You are going shopping for new school clothes. Draw and color some of the clothes and things you would like for school this year.

Answers will vary.

Page 105

Solve these problems.

1. Don was picking apples. He put 36 apples in each box. It took 9 boxes. How many apples did he put in 9 boxes?
36 x 9 = 324

2. Miss Brown has 25 children in her class. She wants to make 5 equal teams for a relay race. How many children will be on each team? **5 children**

3. Ted has saved $9.00 toward buying a new ball. He will get $3.00 today from his father. How much more will he need to buy the $19.95 ball?
$7.95

4. Judy saved 867 pennies in May, 942 in July, and 716 in June. How many pennies did she save in these three months? **2,525** How many more pennies did she save in July than June? **226**

5. Lou needs 5 dozen eggs for a picnic. How many eggs does he need?
60 eggs

6. Fred got a pie for his birthday. He ate 1/2 of the pie that day. He ate 1/4 of it the next day. How much pie he have left? **1/4 pie**

Use the before singular and plural nouns.
Use a or an before singular nouns only.
Use a before words beginning with consonant sounds.
Use an before words beginning with vowel sounds.

Fill in the blanks. Use a, the, or an.

1. **The or An** orange rolled out of my sock.
2. That spider is **a** useful creature.
3. **The** ice fell off the roof.
4. I love to watch **the** parrots when I go to **the** zoo.
5. Have you ever seen **an** octopus?
6. My mother lost **an** earring.
7. My brother, Ron, can play **the or a** drum.
8. **The** floor is covered with newspapers.

SUPER STAR

Page 106

Where would you find the answers to the following questions? Write the name of the reference aid you would use on the line.

| globe | dictionary | encyclopedia |

1. Where is Utah? **globe or encyclopedia**
2. How do they harvest sugar cane in Hawaii? **encyclopedia**
3. Which syllable is stressed in the word profit? **dictionary**
4. What kind of food do people eat in Mexico? **encyclopedia**
5. Which continent is closest to Australia? **globe**
6. Where is the Indian Ocean? **globe or encyclopedia**
7. Who was Thomas Edison, and what did he do? **encyclopedia**
8. What does hibernate mean? **dictionary**
9. Where do you find guide words? **dictionary**
10. Was England involved in the Second World War? **encyclopedia**

Choose the correct spelling for each word. Fill in the circle.

EXAMPLE:
○ babys   ○ babeys   ● babies   ○ babby

1. ○ storys   ● stories   ○ storyes   ○ stories
2. ○ crid   ○ cryed   ● cried   ○ kried
3. ○ seiling   ● ceiling   ○ cieling   ○ sieling
4. ○ certain   ○ sertin   ○ cirtaen   ○ sertain
5. ○ citty   ○ citey   ○ sity   ● city
6. ○ matr   ● matter   ○ mator   ○ mater
7. ● sound   ○ soun   ○ sownd   ○ sounde
8. ○ ucross   ○ acos   ○ ecross   ● across
9. ○ pagge   ○ pag   ● page   ○ jage
10. ○ curcus   ● circus   ○ sircus   ○ circuse

Page 107

Do these problems. Be sure to look at the signs. If you have a calculator, use it to check your answers.

25 − 5 = **20**	28 ÷ 4 = **7**	11 × 11 **121**
6 × 1 = **6**	14 ÷ 7 = **2**	36 − 16 = **20**
36 ÷ 6 = **6**	16 ÷ 6 = **22**	18 ÷ 3 = **6**
5 × 6 = **30**	18 − 8 = **10**	9 × 2 = **18**
17 × 3 = **20**	10 × 3 = **30**	7 × 7 = **49**
11 + 8 = **19**	7 − 3 = **4**	81 ÷ 9 = **9**
19 − 4 = **15**	22 − 2 = **20**	24 + 12 = **36**
4 × 2 = **8**	7 × 6 = **42**	54 ÷ 9 = **6**
9 ÷ 3 = **3**	3 × 7 = **21**	93 − 10 = **83**
12 ÷ 3 = **4**	84 − 80 = **4**	6 × 8 = **48**

Probability and Statistics.

A scientist collected the following data on the length of the whales and dolphins that were studied:

blue whale . . . . 88 feet
humpback whale . . . . 54 feet
gray whale . . . . 39 feet
sperm whale . . . . 35 feet
beluga whale . . . . 13 feet
bottle-nosed dolphin . . . . 9 feet
rough-toothed dolphin . . . . 8 feet
Atlantic spotted dolphin . . . 7 feet
spinner dolphin . . . . 7 feet

- The **range** is the difference between the highest number and the lowest number in the data.
- To calculate the **mean** (or average) add the list of numbers, and then divide by the number of items.
- The **median** is the middle number that appears in the data.
- The **mode** is the number that appears most often in the data.

1. What is the range of the data? **81 feet**
2. What is the median of the data? **13 feet**
3. What is the mode of the data? **7**

Page 108

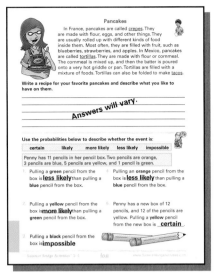

Pancakes

In France, pancakes are called crepes. They are made with flour, eggs, and other things. They are usually rolled up with different kinds of food inside them. Most often, they are filled with fruit, such as blueberries, strawberries, and apples. In Mexico, pancakes are called tortillas. They are made with flour or cornmeal. The cornmeal is mixed up, and then the batter is poured onto a very hot griddle or pan. Tortillas are filled with a mixture of foods. Tortillas can also be folded to make tacos.

Write a recipe for your favorite pancakes and describe what you like to have on them.

Answers will vary.

Use the probabilities below to describe whether the event is:

certain	likely	more likely	less likely	impossible

Penny has 11 pencils in her pencil box. Two pencils are orange, 3 pencils are blue, 5 pencils are yellow, and 1 pencil is green.

1. Pulling a **green** pencil from the box is **less likely** than pulling a **blue** pencil from the box.

- Pulling an **orange** pencil from the box is **less likely** than pulling a **blue** pencil from the box.

2. Pulling a **yellow** pencil from the box is **more likely** than pulling a **green** pencil from the box.

- Penny has a new box of 12 pencils, and 12 of the pencils are yellow. Pulling a **yellow** pencil from the new box is **certain**.

3. Pulling a **black** pencil from the box is **impossible**.

Page 109

Subtract to find the differences.

5,042	2,710	4,200	7,106	3,340	9,824
−1,624	−1,624	−1,122	−2,410	−1,112	−1,224
3,418	**1,086**	**3,078**	**4,696**	**2,228**	**8,600**

6,831	7,605	6,351	8,001	4,232	1,898
−4,560	−1,282	−5,675	−2,381	− 624	− 197
2,271	**6,323**	**676**	**5,620**	**3,608**	**1,701**

2,356	9,010	3,542	5,600	7,575	4,230
−2,147	−2,167	−1,004	−2,983	− 58	−1,606
209	**6,843**	**2,538**	**2,617**	**7,517**	**2,624**

Commas in a series give meaning to a sentence. Put an X next to the correct sentence.

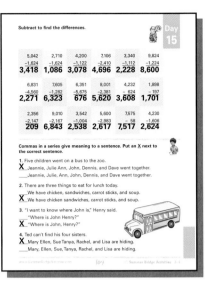

1. Five children went on a bus to the zoo.
X Jeannie, Julie Ann, John, Dennis, and Dave went together.
___ Jeannie, Julie, Ann, John, Dennis, and Dave went together.

2. There are three things to eat for lunch today.
___ We have chicken, sandwiches, carrot sticks, and soup.
X We have chicken sandwiches, carrot sticks, and soup.

3. "I want to know where John is," Henry said.
___ "Where is John Henry?"
X "Where is John, Henry?"

4. Ted can't find his four sisters.
X Mary Ellen, Sue Tanya, Rachel, and Lisa are hiding.
___ Mary, Ellen, Sue, Tanya, Rachel, and Lisa are hiding.

Page 110

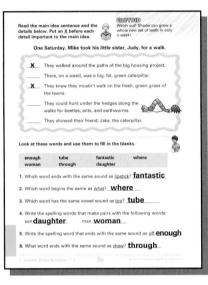

FACTOID
Watch out! Sharks can grow a whole new set of teeth in only a week!

Read the main idea sentence and the details below. Put an X before each detail important to the main idea.

One Saturday, Mike took his little sister, Judy, for a walk.

X They walked around the paths of the big housing project.

___ There, on a weed, was a big, fat, green caterpillar.

X They knew they mustn't walk on the fresh, green grass of the lawns.

___ They could hunt under the hedges along the walks for beetles, ants, and earthworms.

___ They showed their friend, Jake, the caterpillar.

Look at these words and use them to fill in the blanks.

enough	tube	fantastic	where
woman	through	daughter	

1. Which word ends with the same sound as lipstick? **fantastic**

2. Which word begins the same as what? **where**

3. Which word has the same vowel sound as too? **tube**

4. Write the spelling words that make pairs with the following words:
son **daughter** man **woman**

5. Write the spelling word that ends with the same sound as off. **enough**

6. What word ends with the same sound as chew? **through**

Better Bodies

Better Behavior

Up until now, **Summer Bridge Activities**™ has been all about your mind...

But the other parts of you—who you are, how you act, and how you feel—are important too. These pages are all about helping build a better you this summer.

Keeping your body strong and healthy helps you live better, learn better, and feel better. To keep your body healthy, you need to do things like eat right, get enough sleep, and exercise. The Physical Fitness pages of Building Better Bodies will teach you about good eating habits and the importance of proper exercise. You can even train for a Presidential Fitness Award over the summer.

The Character pages are all about building a better you on the inside. They've got fun activities for you and your family to do together. The activities will help you develop important values and habits you'll need as you grow up.

After a summer of Building Better Bodies and Behavior and **Summer Bridge Activities**™, there may be a whole new you ready for school in the fall!

For Parents: Introduction to Character Education

Character education is simply giving your child clear messages about the values you and your family consider important. Many studies have shown that a basic core of values is universal. You will find certain values reflected in the laws of every country and incorporated in the teachings of religious, ethical, and other belief systems throughout the world.

The character activities included here are designed to span the entire summer. Each week your child will be introduced to a new value, with a quote and two activities that illustrate it. Research has shown that character education is most effective when parents reinforce the values in their child's daily routine; therefore, we encourage parents to be involved as their child completes the lessons.

Here are some suggestions on how to maximize these lessons.
- Read through the lesson yourself. Then set aside a block of time for you and your child to discuss the value.
- Plan a block of time to work on the suggested activities.
- Discuss the meaning of the quote with your child. Ask, "What do you think the quote means?" Have your child ask other members of the family the same question. If possible, include grandparents, aunts, uncles, and cousins.
- Use the quote as often as you can during the week. You'll be pleasantly surprised to learn that both you and your child will have it memorized by the end of the week.

- For extra motivation, you can set a reward for completing each week's activities.
- Point out to your child other people who are actively displaying a value. Example: "See how John is helping Mrs. Olsen by raking her leaves."
- Be sure to praise your child each time he or she practices a value: "Mary, it was very courteous of you to wait until I finished speaking."
- Find time in your day to talk about values. Turn off the radio in the car and chat with your children; take a walk in the evening as a family; read a story about the weekly value at bedtime; or give a back rub while you talk about what makes your child happy or sad.
- Finally, model the values you want your child to acquire. Remember, children will do as you do, not as you say.

 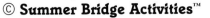

Name _____

Date _____

How I Measure Up!

You will be filling in this page twice—once now and once at the end of the summer to see how you have grown. Have an adult help you measure yourself to fill in the blanks below.

around the neck ___/___

neck to belly button ___/___

around the wrist ___/___

waist to ankle ___/___

foot length ___/___

smile ___/___

shoulder to elbow ___/___

elbow to wrist ___/___

around the waist ___/___

length of longest finger ___/___

around the knee ___/___

around the ankle ___/___

around the neck ___/___

neck to belly button ___/___

around the wrist ___/___

waist to ankle ___/___

foot length ___/___

smile ___/___

shoulder to elbow ___/___

elbow to wrist ___/___

around the waist ___/___

length of longest finger ___/___

around the knee ___/___

around the ankle ___/___

Nutrition

The food you eat helps your body grow. It gives you energy to work and play. Some foods give you protein or fats. Other foods provide vitamins, minerals, or carbohydrates. These are all things your body needs. Eating a variety of good foods each day will help you stay healthy. How much and what foods you need depends on many things, including whether you're a girl or boy, how active you are, and how old you are. To figure out the right amount of food for you, go to http://www.mypyramid.gov/mypyramid/index.aspx and use the Pyramid Plan Calculator. In the meantime, here are some general guidelines.

Your body needs nutrients from each food group every day.

Grains
4 to 5 ounce equivalents each day (an ounce might be a slice of bread, a packet of oatmeal, or a bowl of cereal)

Vegetables
1 1/2 cups each day

Fruits
1 to 1 1/2 cups each day

Oils

Milk
1 to 2 cups of milk (or other calcium-rich food) each day

Meat & Beans
3 to 5 ounce equivalents each day

What foods did you eat today?

Which food group did you eat the most foods from today?

From which food group did you eat the least?

Which meal included the most food groups?

Meal Planning

Plan out three balanced meals for one day. Arrange your meals so that by the end of the day, you will have had all the recommended amounts of food from each food group listed on the food pyramid.

Breakfast

_____
_____
_____
_____
_____

Lunch

_____
_____
_____
_____
_____

Dinner

_____
_____
_____
_____
_____

Meal Tracker

Use these charts to record the amount of food you eat from each food group for one or two weeks. Have another family member keep track, too, and compare.

	Grains	Milk	Meat & Beans	Fruits	Vegetables	Oils/ Sweets
Monday						
Tuesday						
Wednesday						
Thursday						
Friday						
Saturday						
Sunday						

	Grains	Milk	Meat & Beans	Fruits	Vegetables	Oils/ Sweets
Monday						
Tuesday						
Wednesday						
Thursday						
Friday						
Saturday						
Sunday						

	Grains	Milk	Meat & Beans	Fruits	Vegetables	Oils/ Sweets
Monday						
Tuesday						
Wednesday						
Thursday						
Friday						
Saturday						
Sunday						

	Grains	Milk	Meat & Beans	Fruits	Vegetables	Oils/ Sweets
Monday						
Tuesday						
Wednesday						
Thursday						
Friday						
Saturday						
Sunday						

Get Moving!

Did you know that getting no exercise can be almost as bad for you as smoking? So get moving this summer!

Summer is the perfect time to get out and get in shape. Your fitness program should include three parts:

• Get 30 minutes of aerobic exercise per day, three to five days a week.

• Exercise your muscles to improve strength and flexibility.

• Make it FUN! Do things that you like to do. Include your friends and family.

Aerobic

Strength & Flexibility

Fun

If the time you spend on activities 4 and 5 adds up to more than you spend on 1–3, you could be headed for a spud's life!

Couch Potato Quiz

1. Name three things you do each day that get you moving.

2. Name three things you do a few times a week that are good exercise.

3. How many hours do you spend each week playing outside or exercising?

4. How much TV do you watch each day?

5. How much time do you spend playing computer or video games?

You can find information on fitness at www.fitness.gov or www.kidshealth.org

Activity Pyramid

The Activity Pyramid works like the Food Pyramid. You can use the Activity Pyramid to help plan your summer exercise program. Fill in the blanks below.

List 1 thing that isn't good exercise that you could do less of this summer.

1._____

List 3 fun activities you enjoy that get you moving and are good exercise.

1._____

2._____

3._____

List 3 exercises you could do to build strength and flexibility this summer.

1._____

2._____

3._____

List 3 activities you would like to do for aerobic exercise this summer.

1._____

2._____

3._____

List 2 sports you would like to participate in this summer.

1._____

2._____

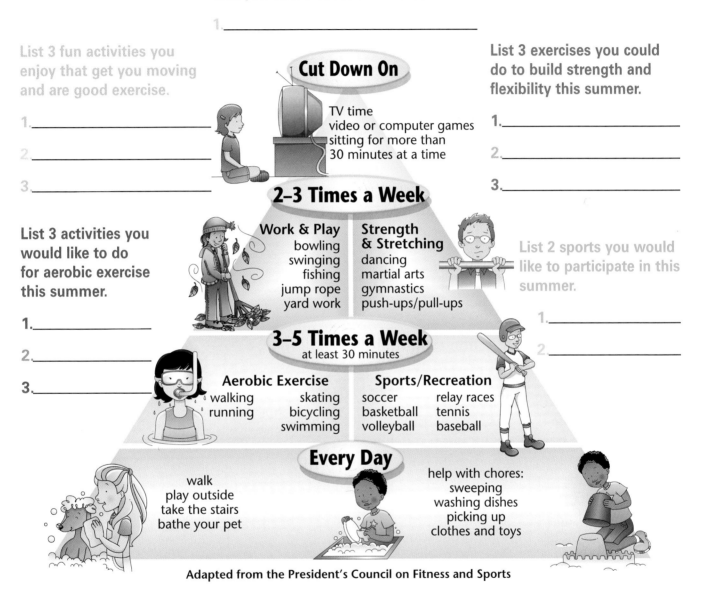

Cut Down On
TV time
video or computer games
sitting for more than
30 minutes at a time

2–3 Times a Week

Work & Play
bowling
swinging
fishing
jump rope
yard work

Strength & Stretching
dancing
martial arts
gymnastics
push-ups/pull-ups

3–5 Times a Week
at least 30 minutes

Aerobic Exercise
walking   skating
running   bicycling
swimming

Sports/Recreation
soccer   relay races
basketball   tennis
volleyball   baseball

Every Day
walk
play outside
take the stairs
bathe your pet

help with chores:
sweeping
washing dishes
picking up
clothes and toys

Adapted from the President's Council on Fitness and Sports

List 5 everyday things you can do to get moving more often.

1._____

2._____

3._____

4._____

5._____

Fitness Fundamentals

Basic physical fitness includes several things:

Cardiovascular Endurance. Your cardiovascular system includes your heart and blood vessels. You need a strong heart to pump your blood which delivers oxygen and nutrients to your body.

Muscular Strength. This is how strong your muscles are.

Muscular Endurance. Endurance has to do with how long you can use your muscles before they get tired.

Flexibility. This is your ability to move your joints and to use your muscles through their full range of motion.

Body Composition. Your body is made up of lean mass and fat mass.

Lean mass includes the water, muscles, tissues, and organs in your body.

Fat mass includes the fat your body stores for energy. Exercise helps you burn body fat and maintain good body composition.

The goal of a summer fitness program is to improve in all the areas of physical fitness.

You build cardiovascular endurance through **aerobic** exercise. For **aerobic** exercise, you need to work large muscle groups at a steady pace. This increases your heart rate and breathing. You can jog, walk, hike, swim, dance, do aerobics, ride a bike, go rowing, climb stairs, rollerblade, play golf, backpack...

You should get at least 30 minutes of aerobic exercise per day, three to five days a week.

You build muscular strength and endurance with exercises that work your muscles, like sit-ups, push-ups, pull-ups, and weight lifting.

You can increase flexibility through stretching exercises. These are good for warm-ups, too.

Find these fitness words.

Word Bank

aerobic	exercise	fat
muscular	flexible	blood
endurance	strength	oxygen
heart rate	joint	hiking

```
u a e y i d t y a g d x p o b
o l s h s t r e n g t h l r c
e w l o o o z v s d m i h d t
g t z w s j o i n t m n k a o
s q a c h i p s a d e t f f m
k c q r x i q f l e x i b l e
e e j o t v k w t e u r g e g
i e s e d r v i n t n f k x o
k e l i d c a d n n e g e j w
u z e d c y u e i g g x i c i
j c i b o r e a h h y w v s i
a m r a a c e m x x x y d i g
f p v n p n d x u s o x e f k
p o c b l o o d e g z a x m c
l e m u s c u l a r m k g i s
```

Your Summer Fitness Program

Start your summer fitness program by choosing at least one aerobic activity from your Activity Pyramid. You can choose more than one for variety.

Do this activity three to five times each week. Keep it up for at least 30 minutes each time.
(Exercise hard enough to increase your heart rate and your breathing. Don't exercise so hard that you get dizzy or can't catch your breath.)

Use this chart to plan when you will exercise, or use it as a record when you exercise.

DATE	ACTIVITY	TIME

DATE	ACTIVITY	TIME

Plan a reward for meeting your exercise goals for two weeks.
(You can make copies of this chart to track your fitness all summer long.)

Start Slow!

Remember to start out slow. Exercise is about getting stronger. It's not about being superman—or superwoman—right off the bat.

Are You Up to the Challenge?

The Presidential Physical Fitness Award Program was designed to help kids get into shape and have fun. To earn the award, you take five fitness tests. These are usually given by teachers at school, but you can train for them this summer. Make a chart to track your progress. Keep working all summer to see if you can improve your score.

Remember: Start Slow!

1. Curl-ups. Lie on the floor with your knees bent and your feet about 12 inches from your buttocks. Cross your arms over your chest. Raise your trunk up and touch your elbows to your thighs. Do as many as you can in one minute.

2. Shuttle Run. Draw a starting line. Put two blocks 30 feet away. Run the 30 feet, pick up a block, and bring it back to the starting line. Then run and bring back the second block. Record your fastest time.

3. V-sit Reach. Sit on the floor with your legs straight and your feet 8 to 12 inches apart. Put a ruler between your feet, pointing past your toes. Have a partner hold your legs straight, and keep your toes pointed up. Link your thumbs together and reach forward, palms down, as far as you can along the ruler.

4. One-Mile Walk/Run. On a track or some safe area, run one mile. You can walk as often as you need to. Finish as fast as possible. (Ages six to seven may want to run a quarter mile; ages eight to nine, half a mile.)

5. Pull-ups. Grip a bar with an overhand grip (the backs of your hands toward your face). Have someone lift you up if you need help. Hang with your arms and legs straight. Pull your body up until your chin is over the bar; then let yourself back down. Do as many as you can.

Respect

Respect is showing good manners toward all people, not just those you know or who are like you. Respect is treating everyone, no matter what religion, race, or culture, male or female, rich or poor, in a way that you would want to be treated. The easiest way to do this is to decide to **never** take part in activities and to **never** use words that make fun of people because they are different from you or your friends.

It's not necessary for eagles to be crows. What I am, I am.
~ Sitting Bull

Word Search

Find these words that also mean *respect*.

Word Bank

honor
idolize
admire
worship
recognize
appreciate
venerate
prize

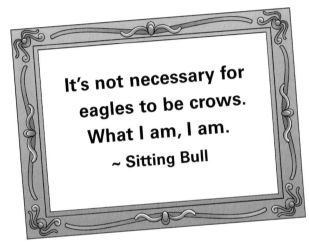

```
m c e t a r e n e v
w j t a h p s e p t
e c a d n n t z i w
z v i m w u k i h r
i e c i h b h n s o
l z e r v b j g r n
o i r e k a u o o o
d r p g m e e c w h
i p p b g c h e r j
q f a b f g u r r z
```

Activity

This week go to the library and check out *The Well: David's Story* by Mildred Taylor (1995). The story is set in Mississippi in the early 1900s and tells about David's family, who shares their well with both black and white neighbors. Be sure to read this book with your parents.

Gratitude

Gratitude is when you thank people for the good things they have given you or done for you. Thinking about people and events in your life that make you feel grateful (thankful) will help you become a happier person.

There are over 465 different ways of saying thank you. Here are a few:

Danke   Toda   Merci   Gracias   Nandri
Spasibo   Arigato   Gadda ge   Paldies   Hvala

Make a list of ten things you are grateful for.

1. _____   6. _____
2. _____   7. _____
3. _____   8. _____
4. _____   9. _____
5. _____   10. _____

A Recipe for Saying Thanks

1. Make a colorful card.
2. On the inside, write a thank-you note to someone who has done something nice for you.
3. Address an envelope to that person.
4. Pick out a cool stamp.
5. Drop your note in the nearest mailbox.

Saying thank you creates love.
~ Daphne Rose Kingma

Friendship

Friends come in all sizes, shapes, and ages: brothers, sisters, parents, neighbors, good teachers, and school and sports friends.

There is a saying, "To have a friend you need to be a friend." Can you think of a day when someone might have tried to get you to say or do unkind things to someone else? Sometimes it takes courage to be a real friend. Did you have the courage to say no?

A Recipe for Friendship

1 cup of always listening to ideas and stories
2 pounds of never talking behind a friend's back
1 pound of no mean teasing
2 cups of always helping a friend who needs help

Take these ingredients and mix completely together. Add laughter, kindness, hugs, and even tears. Bake for as long as it takes to make your friendship good and strong.

I get by with a little help from my friends.
~ John Lennon

Family Night at the Movies

Rent *Toy Story* or *Toy Story II*. Each movie is a simple, yet powerful, tale about true friendship. Fix a big bowl of popcorn to share with your family during the show.

International Friendship Day

The first Sunday in August is International Friendship Day. This is a perfect day to remember all your friends and how they have helped you during your friendship. Give your friends a call or send them an email or snail-mail card.

Confidence

People are **confident** or have **confidence** when they feel like they can succeed at a certain task. To feel confident about doing something, most people need to practice a task over and over.

Reading, pitching a baseball, writing in cursive, playing the flute, even mopping a floor are all examples of tasks that need to be practiced before people feel confident they can succeed.

What are five things you feel confident doing?

What is one thing you want to feel more confident doing?

Make a plan for how and when you will practice until you feel confident.

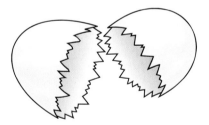

You Crack Me Up!

Materials needed:
1 dozen eggs
a mixing bowl

Cracking eggs without breaking the yolk or getting egg whites all over your hands takes practice.

1. Watch an adult break an egg into the bowl. How did they hold their hands? How did they pull the egg apart?

2. Now you try. Did you do a perfect job the first time? Keep trying until you begin to feel confident about cracking eggs.

3. Use the eggs immediately to make a cheese omelet or custard pie. Refrigerate any unused eggs for up to three days.

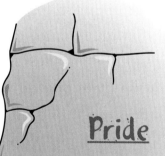

Pride

Never bend your head.

Always hold it high.

Look the world

Right in the eye.

~ Helen Keller

Responsibility

You show **responsibility** by doing what you agree or promise to do. It might be a task, such as a homework assignment, or a chore, such as feeding your fish.

When you are young, your parents and teachers will give you simple tasks like putting away toys or brushing your teeth without being asked. As you get older, you will be given more responsibility. You might be trusted to come home from a friend's house at a certain time or drive to the store for groceries.

It takes a lot of practice to grow up to be a responsible person. The easiest way to practice is by keeping your promises and doing what you know is right.

A parent is responsible for different things than a child or a teenager. Write three activities you are responsible for every day. Then write three things a parent is responsible for every day.

If you want your eggs hatched, sit on them yourself. ~ **Haitian Proverb**

Activity

Materials needed:
21 pennies or counters such as beans, rocks, or marbles
2 small containers labeled #1 and #2

Decide on a reward for successfully completing this activity.
Put all the counters in container #1.
Review the three activities you are responsible for every day.

Each night before you go to bed, put one counter for each completed activity into container #2. At the end of seven days count all the counters in container #2.

If you have 16 or more counters in container #2, you are on your way to becoming very responsible. Collect your reward.

My reward is_____.

Service/Helping

Service is **helping** another person or group of people without asking for any kind of reward or payment. These are some good things that happen when you do service:

1. You feel closer to the people in your community (neighborhood).

2. You feel pride in yourself when you see that you can help other people in need.

3. Your family feels proud of you.

4. You will make new friends as you help others.

An old saying goes, "Charity begins at home." This means that you don't have to do big, important-sounding things to help people. You can start in your own home and neighborhood.

Activity

Each day this week, do one act of service around your house. Don't ask for or take any kind of payment or reward. Be creative! Possible acts of service are

1. Carry in the groceries, do the dishes, or fold the laundry.
2. Read aloud to a younger brother or sister.
3. Make breakfast or pack lunches.
4. Recycle newspapers and cans.
5. Clean the refrigerator or your room.

At the end of the week, think of a project to do with your family that will help your community. You could play musical instruments or sing at a nursing home, set up a lemonade stand and give the money you make to the Special Olympics, offer to play board games with children in the hospital, or pick some flowers and take them to a neighbor. The list goes on and on.

> **All the flowers of tomorrow are in the seeds of today.**
> ~ Indian Proverb

Word Search

Find these words that also mean *service*.

Word Bank		
help	assist	aid
charity	support	boost
benefit	contribute	guide

```
m v l a o d w f d r
c o n t r i b u t e
t b s x c a z v x q
s g p q g w b n y t
i v l y g u v x z i
s n e t e x m n m f
s f h d u d g t e e
a u c h a r i t y n
s u p p o r t u x e
b o o s t g f j g b
```

Honesty and Trust

Being an **honest** person means you don't steal, cheat, or tell lies. **Trust** is when you believe someone will be honest. If you are dishonest, or not truthful, people will not trust you.

You want to tell the truth because it is important to have your family and friends trust you. However, it takes courage to tell the truth, especially if you don't want people to get mad at you or be disappointed in the way you behaved.

How would your parents feel if you lied to them? People almost always find out about lies, and most parents will be more angry about a lie than if you had told them the truth in the first place.

When family or friends ask about something, remember that honesty is telling the truth. Honesty is telling what really happened. Honesty is keeping your promises. *Be proud of being an honest person.*

Write down five feeling words about how you felt when you *weren't* honest or trusted.

1
2
3
4
5

Write down five feeling words about how you felt when you *were* honest or trusted.

1
2
3
4
5

Parent note: Help your child by pointing out times he or she acted honestly.

Count to Ten

Tape ten pieces of colored paper to your refrigerator. For one week, each time you tell the truth or keep a promise, take one piece of paper down and put it in the recycling bin. If all ten pieces of paper are gone by the end of the week, collect your reward.

Most Improved

Honesty is the first chapter in the book of wisdom.
~Thomas Jefferson

My reward is_____.

Happiness

Happiness is a feeling that comes when you enjoy your life. Different things make different people happy. Some people feel happy when they are playing soccer. Other people feel happy when they are playing the cello. It is important to understand what makes you happy so you can include some of these things in your daily plan.

These are some actions that show you are happy: laughing, giggling, skipping, smiling, and hugging.

Make a list of five activities that make you feel happy.

1
2
3
4
5

Bonus!

List two things you could do to make someone else happy.

1._____

2._____

Activity

Write down a plan to do one activity each day this week that makes you happy.

Try simple things—listen to your favorite song, play with a friend, bake muffins, shoot hoops, etc.

Be sure to thank everyone who helps you, and don't forget to laugh!

Happy Thought

The world is so full

of a number of things,

I'm sure we should

all be happy as kings.

~Robert Louis Stevenson

Notes

_____

_____

_____

_____

_____

_____

_____

_____

_____

_____

_____

_____

_____

_____

_____

_____

5 Five things I'm thankful for:

1. _____

2. _____

3. _____

4. _____

5. _____

147

Notes

_____
_____
_____
_____
_____
_____
_____
_____
_____
_____
_____
_____
_____
_____
_____
_____
_____
_____

5 Five things I'm thankful for:

1. _____
2. _____
3. _____
4. _____
5. _____

Multiplication and Division

Developing multiplication and division math skills can be a challenging experience for both parent and child.

- **Have a positive attitude.**
- **Relax and enjoy the learning process.**
- **Keep the learning time short and fun you will get better results.**
- **Review the cards with your child.**
- **Read the front of the card.**
- **Check your answer on the reverse side.**
- **Separate those he/she does not know.**
- **Review those he/she does know.**
- **Gradually work through the other cards.**

These steps will help build your child's confidence with multiplication and division. Enjoy the rewards!

"Teacher, Teacher"

Three or more players.
Each player takes a turn as "Teacher."
The Teacher mixes up the flashcards and holds one card up at a time.
First player to yell out "Teacher, Teacher,"
will have the first chance to give the answer.
If his/her answer is right he/she receives 5 points.
If his/her answer is wrong, he/she will not receive any points.
Move on to the next person until someone answers correctly.
The next round someone else is teacher.
Repeat each round.
Reward the different levels, everyone wins!

Time Challenge

Follow the directions for "Teacher, Teacher" and add a time to it.
Increase the point system to meet the Time Challenge.
Reward the different levels, everyone wins!

0 x 0	0 x 1	0 x 2	0 x 3
4	3	2	1
0 x 4	0 x 5	0 x 6	0 x 7
8	7	6	5
0 x 8	0 x 9	0 x 10	1 x 1
3	2	1	9

$1 \overline{)1}$

0

$1 \overline{)2}$

0

$1 \overline{)3}$

0

$1 \overline{)4}$

0

$1 \overline{)5}$

0

$1 \overline{)6}$

0

$1 \overline{)7}$

0

$1 \overline{)8}$

0

$1 \overline{)9}$

1

$2 \overline{)2}$

0

$2 \overline{)4}$

0

$2 \overline{)6}$

0

2 × 1 7	2 × 2 6	3 × 1 5	3 × 2 4
3 × 3 2	4 × 1 1	4 × 2 9	4 × 3 8
4 × 4 6	5 × 1 5	5 × 2 4	5 × 3 3

$2\overline{)8}$

6

$2\overline{)10}$

3

$2\overline{)12}$

4

$2\overline{)14}$

2

$2\overline{)16}$

12

$2\overline{)18}$

8

$3\overline{)3}$

4

$3\overline{)6}$

9

$3\overline{)9}$

15

$3\overline{)12}$

10

$3\overline{)15}$

5

$3\overline{)18}$

16

5 x 4 1	5 x 5 9	6 x 1 8	6 x 2 7
6 x 3 5	6 x 4 4	6 x 5 3	6 x 6 2
7 x 1 9	7 x 2 8	7 x 3 7	7 x 4 6

$3\overline{)21}$

12

$3\overline{)24}$

6

$3\overline{)27}$

25

$4\overline{)4}$

20

$4\overline{)8}$

36

$4\overline{)12}$

30

$4\overline{)16}$

24

$4\overline{)20}$

18

$4\overline{)24}$

28

$4\overline{)28}$

21

$4\overline{)32}$

14

$4\overline{)36}$

7

$\begin{array}{r} 7 \\ \times\,5 \\ \hline \end{array}$	$\begin{array}{r} 7 \\ \times\,6 \\ \hline \end{array}$	$\begin{array}{r} 7 \\ \times\,7 \\ \hline \end{array}$	$\begin{array}{r} 8 \\ \times\,1 \\ \hline \end{array}$
4	3	2	1
$\begin{array}{r} 8 \\ \times\,2 \\ \hline \end{array}$	$\begin{array}{r} 8 \\ \times\,3 \\ \hline \end{array}$	$\begin{array}{r} 8 \\ \times\,4 \\ \hline \end{array}$	$\begin{array}{r} 8 \\ \times\,5 \\ \hline \end{array}$
8	7	6	5
$\begin{array}{r} 8 \\ \times\,6 \\ \hline \end{array}$	$\begin{array}{r} 8 \\ \times\,7 \\ \hline \end{array}$	$\begin{array}{r} 8 \\ \times\,8 \\ \hline \end{array}$	$\begin{array}{r} 9 \\ \times\,1 \\ \hline \end{array}$
3	2	1	9

$5\overline{)5}$	$5\overline{)10}$	$5\overline{)15}$	$5\overline{)20}$
8	49	42	35
$5\overline{)25}$	$5\overline{)30}$	$5\overline{)35}$	$5\overline{)40}$
40	32	24	16
$5\overline{)45}$	$6\overline{)6}$	$6\overline{)12}$	$6\overline{)18}$
9	64	56	48

9 × 2	9 × 3	9 × 4	9 × 5
7	6	5	4
9 × 6	9 × 7	9 × 8	9 × 9
2	1	9	8
10 × 1	10 × 2	10 × 3	10 × 4
6	5	4	3

$6\overline{)24}$

45

$6\overline{)30}$

36

$6\overline{)36}$

27

$6\overline{)42}$

18

$6\overline{)48}$

81

$6\overline{)54}$

72

$7\overline{)7}$

63

$7\overline{)14}$

54

$7\overline{)21}$

40

$7\overline{)28}$

30

$7\overline{)35}$

20

$7\overline{)42}$

10

10 × 5	10 × 6	10 × 7	10 × 8
7	6	5	4
10 × 9	10 ×10	7)49	7)56
2	1	9	8
7)63	8)8	8)16	8)24
6	5	4	3

$8 \overline{)32}$	$8 \overline{)40}$	$8 \overline{)48}$	$8 \overline{)56}$
80	70	60	50
$8 \overline{)64}$	$8 \overline{)72}$	$9 \overline{)9}$	$9 \overline{)18}$
8	7	100	90
$9 \overline{)27}$	$9 \overline{)36}$	$9 \overline{)45}$	$9 \overline{)54}$
3	2	1	9

$9\overline{)63}$	$9\overline{)72}$	$9\overline{)81}$	$10\overline{)10}$
0	0	0	0

$10\overline{)20}$	$10\overline{)30}$	$10\overline{)40}$	$10\overline{)50}$
0	0	0	0

$10\overline{)60}$	$10\overline{)70}$	$10\overline{)80}$	$10\overline{)90}$
		0	0

$1\overline{)0}$

$2\overline{)0}$

$3\overline{)0}$

$4\overline{)0}$

1

9

8

7

$5\overline{)0}$

$6\overline{)0}$

$7\overline{)0}$

$8\overline{)0}$

5

4

3

2

$9\overline{)0}$

$10\overline{)0}$

9

8

7

6